EXPLORING SOCIAL HISTORY : DALIT'S OF NORTH INDIA

EXPLORING SOCIAL HISTORY : DALIT'S OF NORTH INDIA

DR. KESHAV MISHRA

KALPAZ

ISBN: 978-93-5324-975-5 (HB)

First Published, 2023

Published by

Kalpaz Publications
C-30, Satyawati Nagar,
Delhi - 110052
Ph.: 011-47034999, 9811692060
www.kalpazpublications.com
E-mail: kalpaz@hotmail.com

Printed at: Gyan Press, Delhi.

Contents

PREFACE

Exploring Social History "Dalits of North India" is a collection of research papers based on the empirical data collected by late Prof. N. Mishra over a span of more than twenty years. It was 1973 when he went for an extensive fieldwork among the scheduled castes of Darbhanga district. Late Professor L.P. Vidyarthi also joined him in this venture. They had several joint field work in the beginning and wrote several papers and published a monumental book "Harijan Today" in 1977 jointly. He felt the need to pursue researches among the dalits which was less researched as compared to the scheduled tribes. He undertook researches on various scheduled castes and their different aspects of life and discussed them in different seminars and sessions of various societies of Anthropology.

No society is static. The Dalits along with other down trodden communities in India needed drastic change in their socio-economic conditions to sustain their overall style of life. India after gaining Independence initialed movement for the upliftment of these millions of scheduled castes living life of sub-human beings. There were tug of wars between them and the other caste people who used to exploit them. The essays included in this collection is reflective of the situation for that period of time. Thus, readers can get an over view of the various aspect of Dalits through the perusal of these papers. They throw light even on the contemproray context. Etlmographic details presented in these essays will augment the understanding of the unfolding complexities of Dalit Movement. The rise of untouchables from an interest group to a political force needs to be analyzed. The book will help to grasp the process of mobilization and politicizalion both on electoral & cultural front.

Prof. N. Mishra owed a lot to his teacher and guide late Prof. L.P. Vidyarthi for encouraging to do field work among the Harijans and write papers on them. He insisted him to supervise the research-scholars doing researches for the Ph.D. degree on the problems of the Harijans. Prof. Vidyarthi would very fondly call him the Harijan specialist of the Department of Anthropology, Rauchi University and discussed their problems and solutions for inputs to polity making.

This study would not have been possible without the co-operation of the Harijan informants of various areas, who were so keen and serious in their narration. On behalf of late Prof. N. Mishra. I am thankful to all of them.

Prof. Keshav Mishra
Head Dept. of History/FSS
Banaras Hindu University Varanasi

INTRODUCTION

Bihar and Jharkhand are the two medium sized states jointly spreading over a total area of 1,73,876 Sq.Km. The total populations of the two states according to census of 1991 is 8,63,74,465 out of which more than 7,50,00,000 live in rural areas and only 1,13,00,000 are urban.

The undivided State of Bihar ranked third in term of Harijan population. It has a total Harijan population of 1,25,71,700 persons comprising of 23 different scheduled castes, which was 14.51 percent of the total population of the state. But unfortunately, this section of population was very weak socially, economically and educationally.

Socially in Bihar and Jharkhand, Harijans are of the Shudra origin which has the lowest social status in society and which according to Manu, were only to serve the other caste people, these unfortunate people have no right but only duties to serve mostly such work which others cannot do because of indiguity and profaneness associated with all those jobs like scavenging, skinning, washing dirty cloth, removing carcase and brooming. Economically, they are very poor and handicapped. Most of them are landless agricultural labour who are engaged on a nominal daily wage basis. There is lack of proper market for the daily wage earner hence, only a few lucky persons get even this type of job during busy seasons of agricultural operations. A national survey has revealed that 66 percent of the bonded labourers in the country belong to the scheduled castes. Similarly, the percentage of literacy among the Harijans is very low. It is only 10.40 percent among them, which is lower than that of the scheduled tribes of Bihar. Harijans were referred to as Patita Chandala, Achchoota, Antyaja and the like in the various decenial censuses held in the past.The term Harijan is an award given to them by late Mahatma Gandhi, the father of the Nation. The people of upper caste have always treated them with hatred and have maintained certain prejudices against them.Untouchability, unapproachability, unseenability, unreliability and several other social and religious stigma attached to them have kept them at a distance to upper caste people. They were not allowed entry to public well, temple and several other places of common congregation. They were not allowed to chose the names of gods and heros of epics for their children nor they could pick up a name common among the members of upper caste.They were allowed names of vulgar order and one has to affix caste name with the name. All these have a very deep rooted effect on the service type personality formation of the Harijan and this helped the upper caste to exploit them. Thus, it is clear from the perusal of a few foregoing paragraphs that the Harijan of Bihar are mostly illiterate agricultural labourers. Owing to the factors of urbanisation, industrialisation and mechanisation their age old traditional occupations have also lost their scope in the modern age. Thus, the Harijans have to depend upon the upper caste Hindus for their livelihood. They are compelled to work as agricultural labourers in the farms and fields of upper caste landlords. As has been discussed that in the field of agricultural labour there is seldom full employment of entire labour force hence, in rural areas there is a tendency of a surplus of labour supply to its demand. This situation is very advantageous to the employer and dangerously disadvantages for the Harijans.The Harijans have normally hand to mouth economy and if they do not get jobs regularly they have to starve for want of any saving. No credit facility is available to them because they have no asset nor any property to be offered as security for a loan. The upper caste people know all these handicaps of the Harijans and this situation acts as booster for their exploitation and atrocity.The term atrocity, to the best of my knowledge has not been defined by the penal laws, but offences like murder, rape, arson, assault resulting in grievous hurt, and physical injury and other similar crime committed on scheduled castes and tribes may be included in it. Bihar is one of the few states where exploitation and atrocities of the Harijans are at apex. The daily newspapers are the recorders of the fact. A look on any newspaper captures one's eyes on the prominent news published on the front page about the murder, rape, burning, beating and several other tortures given to the members of the Harijan communities.

Atrocities committed on them have social and economic causes at the root, but when it comes to light many more motives are imputed deliberately to confuse the whole story. It has been mentioned earlier that Harijans are by and large landless labourers. Their socio-economic condition is very low which compels them to work in the fields of landed upper caste people on a very low wage which is much lower to the prescribed minimum wage for the agricultural labourers of Bihar. If they demand the payment of higher wage prescribed by the Government, there would be a clash and the Harijans have to pay the price of all such clashes. Land disputes, forcible harvesting of crops, disputes over provision of house sites are some of the common events, when there is open or latent friction between poor and helpless Harijans with the powerful landlords. There are occasions when they resist the practice of untouchability against them or the practice of bonded labour, the vested interest try to cow them down and terrorise them. Another factor responsible for the atrocities is the practice of indiginities to the Harijan women when they try to preserve their self respect and their women's honour this too becomes irritant for the persons of dominant caste and this is another source of atrocities. Another futile source of atrocities pertains to the disputes regarding Government owned lands or ceiling surplus lands alloted by the Government to the Harijans.When they try to take the possession of such lands, the vested interest try to obstruct them. Thus, atrocities are committed when the Scheduled Caste men seek to secure their legitimate rights in various matters.Other factors like provision of house sites and other economic and educational development schemes, aiming at ameliorating the socio-economic conditions of the Harijans causes anger among the upper caste. It has been seen that atrocities on the Harijans have been committed in groups.The land of Bihar which has been famous for so many good and various things, of late has become notoriously in famous for the atrocities on Harijan. This heinous sin has spread in other states of India also but keeping an eye on the size of Harijan population. Bihar may top in Harijan atrocities. Cases of atrocities on Harijans were not unknown under earlier Zamindari system, but their nature and extent were different from the present day. If an individual Harijan was found guilty for some wrong, he alone was punished for this nor even his other family members were even touched. But now a days there are mass atrocities on Harijan on community basis often with the help or connivance of the police.

Caste Structure of Bihar

The social groups in Bihar can be broadly divided into size categories. The upper castes constitute 12.7 percent of total population. The second major social group is known as backwards constitute 48.9 percent population of the state. The Scheduled Castes, a categories consist of 14.5 percent of the total population of Bihar, whereas the Scheduled Tribes account for 8.9 percent of the population. The Muslims account for 12.2 percent and remaining 2.8 percent are made up by mostly Bengalies and others.

Bihar is a caste and faction ridden state. There is growing tension in the rural areas due to dominance of the upper castes together with the ethos of the Zamindari culture. The economic advancement of the backward classes and growing socio-political awareness among the Harijans have aggravated the problem during recent years. It is the upper caste people who own and possess most of the cultivable fertile lands but they depend upon backward and Harijan for the agricultural operation. Majority of these land holders are the supporter of Congress Party a few of them have favoured B.J.P. and Janta Dal also in recent past.

Factionalism in Bihar is thoroughly marked by Casteism. The middle caste or Backward leadership is not aimed at improving the overall status of these, caste in society. Their role is only to attract the votes of their castes which constitutes 48.9 percent for specific faction leaders. This group is heading the Government in Bihar with Shri Laloo Prasad as the Chief Minister of the state.

These are bands of landless agricultural labour. These people in Bihar are coming under the influence of various ideologies from Gandhian to Marxist Leninist. Even after the abolition of Zamindari the overall condition of these people continues to be deplorable. They have been given protection by the Government and agrarian reforms have raised the expectations of these people. They felt that Government was doing some thing for them and as such they should rise and consolidate their position. The local leaders of various parties have given them organisational help and have helped them in demanding proper wages. These leaders have mostly used them as tools to avenge some old enimity from the ex-landlords. After a period of initial mobilisation of the oppressed, collusions took place in many villages and they had fought an unending bloody war. They are fighting for higher wages and higher prices of their products and a small piece of land on which they can construct a house of their own. Their demand appears to be reasonable but mostly they are motivated by some political leader who are mostly invisible and suffer no loss, but the innocent Harijan has to pay the heavy price for this. Several districts of Central Bihar namely, Patna, Gaya, Nalanda and Aurangabad have witnessed bloody war in the recent past.

The Harijans of Bihar live in a part society. They are found all over in Bihar but everywhere they are assigned a social status much lower than a caste or even a tribe. Whereas a scheduled tribe is a dominant group in its homeland and live like a master. But nowhere in India or in Bihar, the scheduled castes live like a master. They could not grow even the way their counterpart scheduled tribe grew. They were not organised hence they failed to get the share alloted to them alongwith the tribes.

They have innumerable problems in their progress but to me there are two main roots of all these problems. The one is the problem of social disability and the other is that of inequality. Social disability refers to a set of values both positive and negative sanctions for and against these poor Harijans which arrests their various freedom. Although the constitution of India guaranties them the right of equality but in fact the Harijans are inequal to other people economically, socially, educationally, ritually, religiously politically and morally. They are called untouchables and are treated as untouchable. Now practice of untouchability is an offence in India. In the urban areas, there has been some change in the attitude of upper caste people towards the untouchables but in the villages in which India lives, there has not been much perceptible change.

People commonly blame the Brahminic caste system for this rise of untouchability but the empirical reality, however does not confirm this notion, for untouchability is not associated with the Hindu alone. It is found among the Muslims. The Buddhists of Ladakh treat the autochthon of the place as untouchables. Even in the tribal societies one may find a group of people relegated to the position of untouchables, and the Mahalis of Chotanagpur may be taken as an example for the same. To me, it is perhaps poverty which is commonly associated with the untouchables and not the caste system as such which makes them untouchables. Also caste system makes occupations hereditary which makes social position static. Thus, those who opted for any unclean occupation of leather work or sweeping has to hold the rank and position permanently.

Dalits of Bihar is an outcome of the rigorous field work and thinking about the problems of the Scheduled Castes of Bihar by an Indian Anthropologist over a span of more than two decades (1973-1994). The author owes a lot to Late Professor L.P. Vidyarthi as a teacher, guide and philosopher and particularly for initiating him to the unexplored field of Harijan research in 1973. The Scheduled Castes of Bihar were not properly researched before that. The present volume is a collection of eleven scientific papers presented to various seminars and annual session of Indian Science Congress and many of them were published in leading Journals of Social Sciences of India. All these papers deal with the problems of Harijans of Bihar. While a few of them analyse and examine their social organisation and adjustment with the upper caste masters, majority of them reveals their problems and sufferings. A brief summary of the papers given below is relevant at this juncture.

Studies on the Scheduled Castes in Bihar' is the first paper in the Collection in which an attempt has been made to present a brief appraisal of all the books published on the Scheduled Castes of Bihar and several unpublished Ph.D. thesis and dissertations. It also provides some very useful information about various names with which these people have been addressed in the past. One finds that they were called as the 'Chandalas' the 'Patitas', the 'Shudras', the 'Unclean castes', the

'Depressed classes', the 'Exterior Castes' and Harijans different period of time in the past. Now they are known as Dalits. It is interesting to note that at the initial stage they were British administrators like Hunter. Delton, Buchanan, Gait, Risley, O' Moley and Grierson who wrote descriptive account on their life and culture either for census or statistics or settlement report or village notes.

The second paper in the collection, 'Some aspects of the Dusadh of Darbharga' is based on a regorous field work done in the villages of Darbhanga district. It begins with the history of the origin of the Dusadh which is numerically second largest in the Scheduled Castes of Bihar, wherein it has been described that they claim their ancestory from Raja Guhil who was a Rajputra by caste. It contains a long list of 24 branches of Galhot who were the children of Guhil and then there are eleven branches of the Dusadh caste. It depicts almost all important aspects of life. After their origin and branches have been analysed their social history in which family, marriage and several other rituals related to life cycle have been discussed. Economic life, political organisation, religious life in details alongwith their rites and beliefs have been dealt in. It is here that several aspects of Raja Salhesh, their supreme God have been discussed at length. Dusadhs are defamed as criminals. It is commonly believed that they are expert thieves and now-a-days they have resorted to dacoity also. Several case studies of thieves are also given here. Many of these have surrendered before police to lead a life of respectable citizen. Their proper rehabilitation may bring peace in the locality.

'Traditional Political Organisation of the Dhobis of Darbhanga' is the third paper of the collection.This is based on the field work of a few villages of Darbhanga in Northern Bihar. This is the fifth largest scheduled caste of the state. In the caste hierarchy. people of this area considered them as the lowest because they washed the impure clothes of all the other scheduled castes. Traditionally, there used to be a caste Panchayat for the Dhobis exclusively, but after the establishment of State Sponsored Gram Panchayat at Kurson, people prefer to go to this panchayat then the old caste panchayat which was known as the Acha-gama Dhobi-Jati Panchayat. Now a days its decisions are binding only for those who are too poor to go even to Gram Panchayat. Thus, gradually the Dhobi caste panchayat which was once so powerful has been now reduced to almost functionally non-existing. The option is left with the Dhobis themselves whether they abandon it or revive the same.

The fourth paper of the collection is Raja Salhesh the Supreme God of the Dusadh : Barari' a Case Study, provides empirical data about the religious life of the Dusadhs of Barars block within the district of Katihar in Bihar. It has been described that the Dusachs have a separate set of divinity headed by Rajaji or Salhesh Maharaj alongwith several other gods and deities worshipped by the members of Upper Castes. They regard Salhesh as their supreme caste daity. In Barari, there is a small Gahbar (temple) of Salhesh made of thatched house in a corner of the village. There are four terracotta images of males and one of female. While Salhesh is seated on an elephant, others stand on their feet. Salhesh is believed to possess divine strength of unmatching nature and is capable of granting good health and sufficient strength to his devotees. The Dusadhs being a band of landless agricultural labourer count on their strength and good health alone by virtue of which they can earn their bread which is possible with the blessing of Lord Salhesh alone.

'Family and Marriage among the pasis of Darbhanga' is the fifth article of the collection where in an empirical study of family and marriage among the Pasi a Harijan community of Darbhanga district in Northern Bihar has been attempted. The paper starts with the stories about the origin. The Pasis have many sub-castes out of which four are found in this area. They follow their traditional occupation of today tapping and all the members of the family participate in the trade. The family is the basic unit of production and by and large there is good understanding and cooperation among the members of the family. The institution of marriage is very important which help them to lead a regular and contented conjugal life. In their economic compulsiveness the husband plays the role of a collector and the wife a seller, and this division of labour acts as a very congenial system to uphold the status of women, while that is lacking among the members of other scheduled castes. Their socio-economic condition is much better than any other Harijan also the degree of untouchability associated with them is much less and food and drink offered by them in the today shop is accepted by all.

The sixth paper of the collection is 'The Musahar and their Deena-Bhadri'. The study based on empirical facts collected from the villages of North Bihar reveals that the Musahars are the third amongst scheduled caste. They are the most primitive people of the locality having several tribal traits. They live a collective life, move mostly in group and prefer to work in group. Their deep dark skin and a typical dialect they speak distinguish them from other Harijan population. They are very primitive people economically, politically and educationally. The religious life of Musahar is also very distinct. They believe in two sets of gods and spirits, the first set is those of upper caste like Ram, Shiva, Durga and Hanuman. They pay respect to them. The second set is those of the gods and deities of the Musahar community of which Deena Bhadri is the supreme. All the Musahan villages have one Deena-Bhadri-Sthan which has a raised platform made of bricks or earth. Two big bamboos poles are fixed in the centre of the platform which is the abode of Deena-Bhadri and it is here that the Ashadhi Puja is celebrated every year collectively. They believe that Deena-Bhadri is omnipresent and capable of protecting them from all the evils.

Economic problems of the 'Scheduled Castes of Bihar' is the seventh paper of this collection. This is a comparative study of the Harijans of two cultural linguistic zones of Bihar-Tribal and Magahi. Five scheduled castes from the tribal zone, the Bhogta, the Panswansi, the Ghasi and the Chamar and four of them from the Magahi zone-the Musahar, the Chamar, the Rajwar and the Dusadh were the representative scheduled castes from each zone. The study reveals that economically the scheduled castes of Chotanagpur are better off than those of Magahi area because a vast majority of them are engaged in self employment as Artisan where as 70 percent of their counterpart in Magahi area fall back on the upper caste people for bread. The social stigma of untouchability attached to them is much rigid in the Magahi area. Similarly, the evil practice of Begar and meagre wage rate fixed in remote are still continuing. Their exploitation at the hands of ex-landlords and Mahajans is more painful and frequent in this area than in the tribal area. But this does not mean that the Harijans of tribal areas much above want. They also suffer from a very low standard of living and several other socio-economic problems suffered by their brethren of Magahi zone.

In the present collection, the eight paper Problems and Prospects of 'Scheduled Castes of Bihar' an attempt has been made to highlight some of the major problems of the Harijans of Bihar. Landlessness is the most serious problem suffered by them. By and large the scheduled castes comprise the band of landless agricultural labour. Others depend on small and marginal farming, fishing, basket making scavenging and other leather work. Almost all of them are below the poverty line in the economic status. A national survey has revealed that 66 percent of the bonded labourers in the country belong to the scheduled castes Untouchability and stigmatization are yet another serious problems which closes many trades in which they could have been absorbed. Their socio economic disability, superstitious belief and practices also work as impediment in their progress. The atrocities and exploitation of Harijans at the hands of upper caste people make them demoralised. The study reveals that the evil practices of Begar, bonded labour, child-labour, the exploitation of female folk for the sex are rampant among the members of the scheduled castes. After India won Independence, there has been consistant efforts by the Governments to solve the problems of scheduled castes. Several legislations have come into effect to put an end to all the problems suffered by them but in actual effect most of these have reduced to paper work.

"Problems of Harijans Child Labourers and their Welfare needs in Bihar" is the ninth paper of this volume wherein several problems of child labourers have been discussed at length. In the beginning the author talks about child labour, child beggar, child kidnapping for ransom, child drug addiction, child abuse, smuggling of child to the Arabian countries for the camel race and the like. It has been observed that thousands of Harijan children work in various carpet factories of U.P. and Bidi making trade all over the country. The condition of Harijan labourers of the carpet centres at Mirzapur and Bhadohi is pitiable. They have to sit in dark stuffy rooms with their legs dangling in the dark mud put in which the loom is anchored. There is no fresh air at this place. The boys remain in a single position for hours on and shoulders and back lunched over the looms, their eyes vide in the dark. They work and sleep in the same rooms. In fact, it is because of their slender and nimble fingers that children are employed on looms. Similarly, brick-kil in is another industry where both boys and girls are engaged. Tea gardens, open mines and quary, hotels and like are the places where they work every where they are over worked under paid and exploited.

"Socio-economic disabilities of the Harijan of Mithila" is the tenth paper of the collection where in the exploitation of the poor Harijan has been dealt in. It has been mentioned that socio-economic disabilities refer to a set of values, negative and positive sanctions for and against sanctions for and against the untouchables of Mithila which prove detrimental to their freedom and negate their equality. The field work for this paper has been done in the villages of Darbhanga among the Chamar, the Mehtar, the Dusadh, the Musahar and the Dhobi. The causes of disabilities have been attributed to the tradition and castes, occupations and purity pollution concept. Since this area has long been in the Maithil Brahminic influence and has not seen the light of industrialisation, disabilities of the worst type giving place to untouchability, stigmatisation and several other ritual taboos are still operative. Efforts have been made to eradicate these social evils by legislation but this has very slow effect. This needs a change of heart for the people of the upper caste to put an end to this blot on the land of videha.

"Atrocities and exploitation of the Harijan of Bihar" is the eleventh paper of this collection which surveys several cases of atrocities committed on the members of the scheduled castes in the state of Bihar. It records the leading cases of Belchi, Dharampur, Bajidpur, Kalia, Mastipur, Prasbigha, Pipra and Gaini in which the Harijans houses were razed, inmates were killed, property burnt, and women were raped. It also reveals that atrocities committed on them have social and economic causes at the root, but when it comes to light, many more motives are imputed deliberately to confuse the whole story. The demand to pay minimum wage prescribed by the Government possession of land alloted to them either for the cultivation or building houses, forcible harvesting of their crops, refusal to do Begari and protecting the female folk from the sexual exploitation by the members of the Upper Caste are some of the causes which infuriate the members of upper caste and they avenge the mute Harijans by committing atrocity on them to teach them lesson so that they behave in the manner, they are forced to behave by the members of the dominating caste of the particular locality. The sin of atrocity has been stopped by the Government but the study reveals that now-a-days there are mass atrocities on Harijans on community basis.

The twelveth and the last paper of the collection, "Agrarian unrest in Rural Bihar provides empirical facts about a situation when the Harijans have mobilised their resources, mustered courage and have organised themselves to counteract the oppression of the Upper Caste people. Initially, the Upper caste people were habituated to keep the Harijans under their boots at this stage, if they rose they were crushed by way of atrocities and these people had to suffer a lot. This study depicts as to how these poor landless Harijans have formed various types of senas (Private Army) like Naxalite, Lalkhandi, Dalit Sena, M.C.C., I.P.F. and the like to fight back the Upper Caste people. The upper caste people have also formed caste army like Savarna Liberation Front, Sunlight, Safalight Kumar Sena, Brahmrishri Sena and the like. Thus, the presence of two sets of Senas confronting each other reminds and cautions the situation of the Mahabharata. Thus, whole of Rural Bihar particularly the Central Bihar is under the grip of an unending unrest. There is one caste conflict at a particular place which has a chain reaction at various places and this goes on rotating having no end in sight. The last life cycle Rituals, Fair and Festival among. the Dalits of Himachal Pradesh is a descriptive study of Dalits of Himachal Pradesh.

1

STUDIES ON THE SCHEDULED CASTES IN BIHAR

Tracing the origin of the Scheduled Castes one has to go back to the origin of caste itself. According to the classical theory of Varna those who sprang from the mouth of the Brahma (Creator) were called the Brahmins, from the arms were called the Kashtriyas, from the things were called the Vaishyas and from the feet were called the Shudras. The Shudras came from the lowest part of the body and hence held the lowest position in the Varna hierarchy. The so-called Scheduled Castes of today belong to the Shudra Varna.

The Scheduled Caste of today have been referred to by the various terms in the early history of India. Whereas, in the Hindu scriptures they have been called as the 'Chandalas', 'Patitas' and the Shudras, in censuses, they have been referred to as "Unclean castes", "Depressed Classes", "Exterior castes" and the like. Since the enactment of the Government of India Act of 1935 they have been consistently referred to as Scheduled castes. Thus, many untouchable castes throughout India were listed in a separate schedule in the Act and this practice was continued in the Constitution of India 1950. The list of Scheduled castes can be altered only by the President of India. The word Harijan (the children of Hari or God) which was awarded by Mahatma Gandhi for the untouchables is almost invariably employed as a synonym for the Scheduled castes, In Bihar, 23 communities have been declared as the Scheduled castes, whose population according to census of 1971, is about 8 million which constitute 14.11 percent of the total population of the State.

Any person who attempts to present an appraisal of the studies in the scheduled castes of Bihar is attacked by many faced problems some of which are very grave. To my mind, non-availability of literature for the said research is perhaps the greatest of all. If one seeks back into the history of the studies in the Scheduled castes one is bound to be disappointed as there is no systematic account on their life and culture. The earlier information about them is sporadic, sketchy and fragmentary, recorded in the villages notes, official papers, census and survey reports, district gazetteers and the reports of the Commissioner of the Scheduled Castes and the Scheduled Tribes. Frequent references of them do occur in the travel account, in the report of the social workers, reformers and the like. It appears that Francis Buchanan who wrote four volumes about the land and people of Bihar in general and the districts of Patna, Bhagalpur, Purnea and Shahabad in particular had some anthropological insight in the treatment of the problems of the scheduled castes. Dr. Francis Buchanan under the orders of the Governor-General in Council surveyed the districts mentioned above along with other districts then forming part of the presidency of Bengal during the year 1807-14. The results of the survey were transmitted to England in 1816 and in 1838. It was published first in Eastern India which was later on published by the Bihar and Orissa Research Society in the year 1928.

Buchanan's volumes are pionnering in may ways. It goes without saying that they contain the first hand account of the Scheduled castes in as early as 1807. Thus, these informations about their marriage customs social position etc., function as bench line data for any scientific research on them.

Dalton's "Descriptive Ethnology on Bengal" published in 1872 may be regarded yet another source of information of the Scheduled castes and the Scheduled tribes in general. As is vivid from the very title of the book it is a descriptive account of some of them. There are some very brief ethnographic notes about these very little known Scheduled tribes and castes. This study, despite the limitations, has helping the researchers like the Polar star since more than a century.

W.W. Hunter's "A Statistical Account of Bengal" published in 1877 may also be regarded as a mile-stone in this regard. Though we do not get a systematic account of any Scheduled caste in it, it does preserves glimpses of their life. It contains the ethnical division of the people,

Emigration and Immigration lists of castes, religious division of the people, village institutions, material culture, agriculture and commerce and many other useful information important from anthropological point in view.

Risley's "Tribes and Castes of Bengal" published in two volumes in the year 1891 may be regarded as monumental work for these volumes were the first to have anthropological insight. The author tried his best to touch important aspects of all the major Scheduled castes and tribes.

After the works of Risley there is rather a big gap for about thirty years as there is no published work about them except the census reports.

In the year 1920, S.C. Roy published his monograph on the Bhuiyas which may be regarded as the master piece in the germane field. It comprises of social organisation, kinship system, marriage, inheritance, birth, childhood, puberty customs, death and death rites, and the like. S.C. Roy, as the father of Indian Anthropology, may be regarded as the first Indian to have taken the cause of the scheduled castes and have written a volume on them.

G.W. Briggs published his monumental book "The Chamar" in 1920. Though this was mainly based on the field work carried on among the Chamars of U.P., there are several references of the Chamars of Bihar also in this book. This is a rare work and the first full length monograph ever written on a Scheduled caste.

Grierson "Bihar Peasant life" published in 1926 is yet another book where we find some information about the condition of some of the Scheduled castes in Bihar.

"The Myth of Caste System" by N. Prasad published in 1957 may be regarded as a wonderful work on the scheduled castes of Bihar. Mr. Prasad has extensively worked on the Scheduled castes and has enriched the poor store of the study among the Scheduled castes.

R.R. Diwakar's "Bihar Through the Ages" published in 1959 may be taken as eventful for he has tried to analyse the social system of the various tribes and castes of Bihar right from the early vedic period till the book was published, Diwakar deserves congratulations for he could accommodate even the untouchables.

"Inside Bihar" by P.C. Roy Choudhary published in 1962 is very informative for the author has very carefully described the affairs of the scheduled castes along with the Upper castes. This work is specially useful for the researches of Bihar, particularly those interested in the study of caste system and the like.

S.D. Prasad, the then Superintendent of the Census operations of Bihar took some special interest in the census of 1960 by providing a section of the ethnographic notes and also a few village studies in the forms of monographs. These ethnographic notes and monographs also depicted the cultural life of the Scheduled caste people and are useful for the obvious reasons.

Contribution of Ranchi University Anthropology Deptt. in the Scheduled caste studies in Bihar deserves specific mention. The post graduate teaching in Anthropology was started here in 1953 in Ranchi College which was then a constituent unit of the Bihar University. On inception of the University of Ranchi in 1960, this automatically, became the University Deptt. of Anthropology Ranchi University Ranchi. This Deptt. was mainly engaged in the researches among the Scheduled Tribes which were then very little known. We do not have a monograph on the scheduled castes either by the Post-graduate students or any other scholar before 1965. To the best of my knowledge, it was in the village of Amanari in the district of Hazaribagh that a few students carried on their field work on the Bhuiyas and the Chamars and wrote monographs on them in 1965. Again in 1969 a few students worked among the Chamars and the Musahars of Madhubani in the district of Darbhanga. In the year 1972 Arun Kumar, a student of this department wrote a dissertation "Studies on Scheduled Castes in India" in which he has devoted considerable space on the Scheduled castes of Bihar too.

The Scheduled caste studies in Bihar particularly by the Department of Anthropology, Ranchi University felt a bomp when a batch of about 20 Post-graduate students with two teachers (Dr. N. Mishra and Dr. P. D. Sharma) were sent by Professor Vidyarthi to carry on field work among the Scheduled castes of Darbhanga in the year

1973. Prof. Vidyarthi also visited the camp and supervised the work. The two teachers looked after the social and physical anthropological aspects of the scheduled castes respectively. The findings of the researches thus carried out are given in a few following paragraphs.

The findings of physical Anthropological researches were that the Dusadhas had no sociological religions with the tribals. On the other hand, they were closer to clean Hindus in general. However, this could not be clearly established that they had the same blood type as that of the Kshtriyas. It was claimed by them that they were Gahlot Rajputs and their ancestors migrated from Rajasthan to Gaya and then settled in various parts of North Bihar.

The unit of the social anthropology students under the leadership of Dr. Mishra covered as many as five Scheduled castes of Darbhanga. Whereas, six students carried on field work on the different aspects of the Dusadhas, rest of the four students collected materials for a total monographic studies among the Pasi, the Dhobi, the Chamar and the Mehtar. Here a few lines about the findings of the researches of individual students merit attention.

Miss Indira Bhattacharya wrote a beautiful report on the social life of the Dusadhas. She has very carefully collected materials about the family marriage, kinship system, rites de-passage, inter and intra caste relationship socialisation, education and Sanskritisation. The treatment of data in the report is good and the style of narration is excellent.

Miss Bulbul Roy wrote on the "Religious life of the Dusadhas". This is also a good report because it deals with the Gods and Goddesses of the little tradition. The Dusadhas took Lord Salhesh as their supreme God. They worship various dieties in different months. The impact of the higher form of Hinduism has also been established.

Miss Bandna Bhattacharya wrote a report on the "Political life of the Dusadhas". She has recorded the biographies of the political leaders. Her treatment of the Baisi Gram Panchayat and the proceedings of the Panchayat and the like shows her rare insight into the political problems of the Dusadhas of Darbhanga.

Mr. Keshav Singh collected materials about "the life cycle of the Dusadhash". This report is very informative because it contains a chapter about the origin of the Dusadhas also His treatment of the various sub-castes of the Dusadhas is excellent.

Two other students namely Miss Sajda Begum and Miss Igmis Tirkey who collected materials on "The role of Dusadh Women" and "The Economic life of Dusadh" could not pull on their studies due to domestic problems. As such they could not write the reports on the topics offered by them.

Thus, from the perusal of the foregoing few paragraphs it is vivid that the team of the social anthropologists collected materials about every aspects of the Dusadhas of Darbhanga during 1973 field work camp.

As has been mentioned earlier, four, out of ten students offered to write monographs on the Pasi, the Dhobi, the Chamar and the Mehtar, respectively. It is high time that a few paragraphs are written about them individually.

Mr. B.M. Mukherjee wrote a monograph on the Pasi of Darbhanga. This is really a wonderful work because of the richness of date and their analysis. In addition to a beautiful introduction and well balanced conclusion, this report contains chapters on the Social Organisation life cycle, main and subsidiary Economy division of labour, material culture, in debtedness, standard of living, caste panchayats, gods and dieties, beliefs and rituals with festivals and problems and prospects. Thus, it is explicit from the perusal of the contents that Mr. Mukherjee has not left any stone unturned to make the report a full monographic study of the Pasi. Where there is caste hierarchy among the Harijan, the Pasi tops the list. That even the elean caste people take Tari and also Chakhana at the hands of the Pasi on the plea that intoxicant recognises no caste are some of the rare facts revealed in this the work.

Although every page of the report of Mr. Mukherjee is useful, yet the chapter on "Problems and prospect" is specially significant where the author has discussed how they are sporadically scattered in far off places which work as impediments in organising them, socially and politically. The literacy rate was reported to be low. They suffered from a peculiar problem of transition. Many of them adopted higher philosophy of the Maithil Brahmins, the dominant caste of the area, in a bid to go up in the caste hierarchy, thus treating themselves above the other co-caste men in social and religious performances. On the other hand, the clean Hindus were reluctant in accepting them in their mainstream. It goes without saying that the Pasis of Darbhanga were slightly better off socially, educationally, Political and also economically and that might be the main cause for their isolation from the other Scheduled castes in general including the Pasis of rural area.

Mr. J. Lugun wrote a monographic report on the hobi. This report also contains almost every aspect of Dhobi life. Socially, the Dhobis were said to be on the lowest rung as they washed the blood stained and polluted clothes of the menses of the Chamars and the Mehtars. Economically they were landless labour. Thus, washing was the only source of their income they were badly indebted to the Mahajans. There was a caste Panchayat to look after the social norms of the caste Although they were untouchables, yet as their services were of essential nature people did not abhor them to the extent of the Chamars and the Mehtars.

Mr. Parminar Lakra wrote a full length monographic report on the Chamars of Darbhanga.The content of his report and the scheme of the chapterisation are the same as those of Mr. Lugun. But the Chamars were worse than the Pasis and the Dhobis, socially and economically. The Chamars had occupation of skinning and ate beef and as such they carried stigma. Shoe polish and repair was their main source of livelihood and by and large they were also landless.

Mr. Mathiya Oraon did monographic study of the Mehtar of Darbhanga. This study is based on the field work carried on by him mainly in the twin villages-Laxmisagar and Choora Bhathi of Darbhanga in Bihar. This is a very informative report.

It was reported that originally the Mehtars lived at Lalbagh but in a bid of the expansion of the palace of Raj Darbhanga, these Mehtars had to migrate and settle at Choora Bhathi and Laxmisagar villages provided by the Maharaja in 1942-43.

The caste of Mehtar was divided into three endogamous groups. 1. Rahut, 2. Hari and 3. Mehtar. The Rahut was the top most, the Hari in between and the Mehtar was the lowest, in social position.However in the matters of other spheres of life, this division of the caste was ignored and there was full cooperation among the members of the caste.

In the matters of Rites-de-passage they were governed by the Mithila style of life and they tried to follow the high model of Maithil Brahmin despite the economic impediments in doing so. There was better deal for an expectant mother. She was expected to do light job and take better food. Every one had kind words for her in the early months sexual intercourse was avoided as that might cause abortion. She was not allowed to go out alone late at night. There was taboo in her touching the dead body and going to the cremation ground. With regard to their marriage it was interesting to note that there was a caste panchayat for the members of the Mehtar caste which had framed certain codes for marriage in the month of December, 1971 which had 20 following section:

1. These codes would apply uniformly on all the members of the castes.
2. There would be only adult marriage.
3. The system of second marriage (gawna) would be abandoned hence forth.
4. The bride will have to remain in the house of her husband at least for about 40 days in her first visit.
5. There would not be Gawna any more.
6. In no case the number of the Barat would cross the limit of 27 persons.
7. The marriage celebrated by the custom of Bar-Puja will be accepted as the only prescribed method of the Mehtar marriage.
8. The Bar-Puja will be celebrated at the house of the groom in which the bride party will offer Rupee one and one piece of

Dhotee, but, in no case the number of party will exceed 5 persons.

9. After the Bar-puja has been celebrated, only in the case of some incurable disease this marriage could be abandoned.
10. Giving or accepting Tilak (dowry) is totally banned.
11. Separation or divorce could be possible under the Special Marriage Act.
12. There would be only vegetarian dishes on the eve of marriage and puja.
13. The Barat party will be served with only two meals.
14. The bride party will offer only two pieces of clothes besides the garments of the bride.
15. Only one party can arrange for the band party and the other one with a dance party if one so likes. But in no case loud speakers will be allowed.
16. The widow remarriage will be celebrated in presence of 5 Panchas.
17. The widow remarriage will be practised.
18. There would not be Barat or any transaction in the widow remarriage.
19. Only monogamy will be acceptable.
20. Any person found guilty of violating the codes mentioned above would be liable for a fine ranging from Rs. 125 to Rs. 500/.

which will be deposited in the treasury of the Mehtar Caste Panchayat. Thus, it is clear from the perusal of the codes of the Mehtar Caste Panchayat in connection with marriage that good sense has prevailed among the members of the scavenging caste who are on the lowest rung in the social hierarchy of Mithila, by abandoning the pomp and show in celebrating the marriages. As is vivid from the careful observation of their economic life, they are the worst hit people, who are half fed and ill clad even after carrying night soil in buckets over their heads. They are below subsistence level, and hence these codes have proved as boons for the poor Mehtars of Darbhanga. They were by and large happy about these codes regulating their marriage celebration effectively in proper manner.

The occupation of the Mehtar could be well categorised under four following heads :

1. Cleaning and Scavenging
2. Domestication of swine
3. Picking burnt coal by rail tracks,
4. Making Bidi on contract basis

1. Cleaning and Scavenging were the main occupation of the Mehtars. By and large every able and desirous person was employed by the local municipality. The ladies were engaged for carrying the night soil whereas the gents cleaned the roads and drains. They also carried the dead animal. A few of them got part time jobs of brooming and cleaning in the local offices and business installations. Thus, by and large they were engaged to clean the filth which no other person would like to do. The importance of the services they render can best be evaluated when there is a strike of the scavengers that too in the traditional town of Darbhanga where most of the houses had service latrine.
2. Demestication of swine was the main subsidiary occupation of the Mehtars of Darbhanga. The Mehtars lived in a very inhospitable and insanitary condition. The swine helped them in cleaning the filth partially. Mostly old persons who could not do any hard work would go to graze the pigs assisted by children. They never offered any food or grain to pigs. The pigs were sold for about Rs. 100/- or more. Thus, they supplemented their budget with the sale proceeds.
3. Small children and old women were kept busy in picking the burnt coal on the rail track. The lion's share of the coal

collected in this way was sold for Rs. 2 to 3 per basket whereas a small quantity of it was used for the domestic consumption. This was also one of the subsidiary sources of income for the poor Mehtars.

4. The fourth source of income for them was from making Bidi for the local Bidi merchants. It was noticed that they got Rs.4/- per thousand as labour charges for making Bidis. They got raw materials from the merchants for whom they worked. Thus they earned something in the leisure.

Indebtedness among the Mehtars was yet another interesting point in the present study. Landless labour as they were and the meagre income that they had, they were compelled to live hand to mouth. They did not have saving worth the name. As such on the eve of marriage, illness, death and festivals they always ran for some loan at exorbitant rate of interest. There were two ways of obtaining loan either by mortgaging some golden and silver ornaments or brass rice plate etc. In case when golden or silver ornaments have been mortgaged, the rate of interest is 20 per rupee per month and in case of the brass utensils this goes to 30 paise per rupee per month. Thus, the rate of the interest was so high and the calculation of interest so cumbersome that seldom a Mehtar could repay the debt and could get back the ornament once mortgaged to the Mahajan. In cases when nothing was mortgaged the rate of interest was an anna per rupee per month which if calculated would come to 75 percent.

Problems of the Mehtar

The study of the problems of the Mehtars of Darbhanga deserves specific mention here. Some of the problems faced by them are all India problems while local problems like those of housing and untouchability were specific problems. The district of Darbhanga in general is a flood affected one. Marshy land and moors are the common features. The Mehtars are the untouchables here. They were therefore allotted land by the Raja of Darbhanga by the side of moor which is full of water and a water born creepers and vegetation and hence den of snakes and mosquitoes. Their poor economic condition did not allow them to build pucca houses. During rainy season particularly when the river Bagmati was flooded, most of their houses collapsed, rendering them homeless. Seldom a Mehtar had any cot to sleep or any other furniture to sit on. They did not have a cemented floor of the house and slept on a thin mat spread over the floor. Put the floor was always moist. As such they suffered from various diseases like cold and cough, gout, rheumatic fever and the like. The problems of drinking water was very serious. They were not allowed on the wells used by the higher castes. There was no municipal water tap in the locality inhabited by them.The filthy surroundings always made them the first prey in case of outbreak of the epidemics.

It has been mentioned elsewhere that the year 1973 was significant for the Scheduled Caste studies. Prof. Vidyarthi felt the negligence of the study of Scheduled castes and made up his mind to replenish the lag. He encouraged Shri B. M. Mukherjee to write an M.A. dissertation on the scheduled caste. Shri Mukherjee took the challenge and prepared a synopsis on the comparative study of the Scheduled castes of Bihar under my supervision. Shri Mukherjee had to face chains of problems and non-availability of literature was the most difficult problem which he managed to overcome by visiting the National Library of Calcutta.

Coming to the dissertation entitled "A comparative study of Scheduled castes in three culture linguistic zones of Bihar", One is amazed to find that this concept of three culture linguistic zones established by Prof.Vidyarthi has been taken as the unit of study. The author mainly used the published work as the sources of materials but had to do some field work also in the villages of Mithila from where he could get nothing in black and white. Regarding the significance of the study the author writes. "The Scheduled castes of India present many faceted problems before us they suffer very much from the social isolation and stigmatisation, their traditional occupations being derogatory. As such it entails many more disabilities. They have been neglected for many decades and the anthropologists have paid very little or no attention towards these people. The Harijan community deserves more attention than those of the so-called primitives".

The main objectives of the dissertation are to test seven following hypotheses by the author :

1. It is concerned that geographical environment, caste dominance and language may be responsible to determine the culture of the people concerned.
2. Though the culture of a particular linguistic zone may be homogeneous, there may be some distinctive feature of the minority group.
3. This also assumes that the scheduled castes are to some extent homogeneous though they are hetrogeneous groups.
4. It has also been an effort to see the proximity of the Scheduled castes culture with that of the aboriginal inhabitants.
5. Industrial progress of the state is also responsible for the change in the way of living of the people and hence it has been many effort to test the assumptions.
6. So far no work has been done in the direction of finding out a middle range unit of analysis between the linguistic zones of Bihar. This is an attempt to see as to how far such cultural regions can be determined on the basis of language. There is an homogenity in terms of the ethnolinguistic traditions of the people in general and scheduled castes in particular. It is also an attempt to test the theories given by Grierson as there are ethnic differences between the Maithili, Magahi and tribal people. The present study is a guide to know as to how far the ancient history of the region, traditions of which it retains to the pressent day is responsible for moulding and shifting its people. Mithila, a country under the domination of those Brahmins exclusively devoted to orthodox religion, has a metaphysical bias and this idea greatly dominates the Scheduled castes of that zone. It is presumed that the scheduled castes in Mithila are a little apart from those of the Magahi and Tribal region.

7. The very idea of impact of the Adivasi on Scheduled castes inhabiting the tribal zone may very hopefully lead to the study of other linguistic zones and this calls for a comparison between the linguistic zones in relation to the culture of the scheduled castes.

The content analysis of the dissertation reveals that this is divided into seven chapters. The author has taken the economic life in the first chapter where he mentions that there are the bands of landless agricultural labourers. Their subsistance is conspicuously poor and they virtually lead a life of sub-human by the world standard. By and large they are indebted to the Mahajans and Sahukars and thus lead a life of hell.

The second chapter portrays the social life with their social organisation and different customs related to the rites de passage. Their adherence to the old customs, superstitions and attitude towards the new changes have also been analysed here.

The third chapter comprises of the political organisation based on the caste panchayats. Solidarity and unity in collusion with village politics is a distinctive feature of this chapter.

In the fourth chapter, the readers will find information about the religious life of the scheduled castes. Their beliefs and practices are also analysed here in this chapter.

The fifth chapter has been devoted to inter group relationship among the Scheduled castes as well as with the higher castes. The change of outlook in the realm of social relationship has also been dealt with here.

Problematic study of the Scheduled castes has been the theme of the sixth chapter. Their general problems problems of social economic and political disabilities have been very carefully analysed here. The author has taken pains in evaluating the meagre ameliorative measures initiated by the Governments.

The last chapter contains the summary and conclusions of the work. One wonders as to how the author has missed to write the results of the testing of the hypothesis in the conclusion. But for this minor point Shri Mukherjee deserve congratulations for writing such an informative dissertation on the scheduled castes of Bihar.

It has been mentioned elsewhere that Prof. Vidyarthi wanted to fill up the vacant treasure of the knowledge about the scheduled castes. He moved the U.G.C. with a proposal to sanction funds for a research project namely, "The Scheduled castes in Bihar". The U.G.C. sanctioned Rs.10,000 for the said project during 1973 - 75. Two Research Assistant Shri D. C. Munda and Shri M.P. Srivastava were appointed. Dr. L. P. Vidyarthi and Dr. N. Mishra were appointed Honorary Director and Dy. Director of the project. The two assistants were made in charge of the field work among the scheduled castes of the tribal and theMagahi zones respectively. The report of the project was submitted in 1976.The success of the project is praise worthy because the report has been published in a book form entitled "Harijans Today" by Dr. L. P. Vidyarthi and Dr. N. Mishra in August 1977 by Classical Publications of Delhi. This book runs into 224 pages. The book in question is the outcome of rigorous field work by the research scholars and investigations along with the intensive supervision of the authors. The work records and presents a new approach to the analysis of the political, social, economic, cultural and religious aspects of lived of the still unexplored Scheduled castes in Tribal as well as in Magahi zones of Bihar.

The authors have done pioneering work by studying all the aspects of these so-called Harijans in connection with their interaction with wider context. Special attention has been focussed on social disabilities economic inequality, landlessness, indebtedness, frequent and seasonal migrations. The hierarchical position, different kinship, usages, panchayats, and the impacts of Sanskritisation in religious life of the Harijans have been systematically analysed. Even Government help through welfare programme in relation to their hygiene and sanitation has been critically attempted.

The book so laboriously produced with such a mass of facts and figures makes surprisingly easy reading and as in eye opener for all the scholars and researchers in the development of the rural work.

The year of 1875 was very fruitful for the Scheduled caste studies in Bihar. The Department of Anthropology led by Prof. Vidyarthi who was also the General Secretary to the Council of Social and Cultural Research, Bihar and Editor of the Journal of Social Research decided to publish a special number of Jornal of Social Research exclusively on the Scheduled castes. Papers on the Scheduled castes were invited for the special number of and the September Issue of 1975 Vol. XVIII No.2 was published as the special number on Scheduled castes. Altogether thirteen research papers were included in this volume out of which five papers were about the scheduled castes of Bihar. It will not be out of place to mention a few lines about the individual papers.

K. N. Sahay wrote on "Eradication of Untouchability and the caste system". The author has very correctly differentiated between the caste system and untouchability. He is of the opinion that it is not practical to abolish the caste system for obvious reasons but the abolition of untouchability is both possible and proper Concludingly he has suggested five measure to eradicate the untouchability which are invaluable.

N. Mishra chose to write on "Some aspects of the Dusadh of Darbhanga". The Dusadhs of Darbhanga are notorious and defamed Scheduled caste.The author has taken pains to do field work among them and has tried to understand as to what makes them criminals. Lack of job opportunities, absence of any traditional occupation and exploitation by the persons of high landed caste and harassment by the police officials have rather compelled them to become criminals. They claim that they are decendants of king Goha, a Kshtriya and try their best to regain the lost Kshtriya Varna. But during the dazzle of day, higher caste person would not concede their demand. Thus, at night they rule. They try to avenge. Thus, they plunder, loot and even kill the rich persons at night. Now they are tried of their lives of criminals. In response to Jaiprakash Narayan's movements of arms surrender many of them have voluntarily surrendered for a respectful and peaceful life and future of their children . 'Scheduled caste student of College' by Sachidanand is a very interesting paper. The Chamar, Dushadh, Dhobi and Pasi account for 95 percent of the college going students. More than 75 percent students offer Arts course. Since most of the students come from very poor homes, they have to spend quite some time in domestic work. This paper is very informative about the aspirations and attitudes of the Scheduled caste students. 35 percent of them want to continue till they complete the Masters level and 16.4 percent would like to finish high professional courses like M.B.B.S. B.Sc. (Eng) or study upto the Doctor's level.

Regarding their knowledge of reservation of posts in government service and their aspirations it has been mentioned that 43 percent of them aspire to become high govt. officers in the administration or in the police or the armed forces. Only 25 percent because of their poor academic achievements or taste in getting jobs, would like to be satisfied with low paid jobs of teachers clerks, village level workers etc. Almost every one has given the first preference to govt. jobs where posts are reserved for them.

'Economic problems of the Scheduled castes of Bihar' is another very useful and informative research paper written jointly by Dr. L.P. Vidyarthi and Dr. N. Mishra, it is a comparative study of the Scheduled castes of the tribal and the Magahi zones. The authors have very correctly observed that the Scheduled castes in general are landless agricultural labourers. Economically the scheduled castes of Chotanagpur are better off than those of Magahi area. A vast majority of them are self employed as artisans whereas more than 70 percent of their counterparts in Magahi area fall back on the landed upper caste people. The economic life of these people is more insecure because of their casual employment on the daily wage system. The wage paid to them is too meagre to maintain them. Above 45 percent of them are indebted to village Mahajans and pay an exorbitant rate of interest.

The 5th and last paper in the special number is of Shri B.M. Mukherjee on "A short note on marriage customs among the untouchables of Mithila Pasi- A case study." This paper is based on the field-work of the author. The author has very carefully observed the customary rites among the Pasi of Darbhanga and has written a beautiful account of the marriage customs in general and Uthangar, Ghunghati Nirik-chhan, Kanyadan, Kumari Lahchha, Nak-bedi, Sindhursdan, Kohbar, and Dooragman in particular. The author has rightly observed the impact of the culture of Maithil Brahmins on the marriage rites of the Pasi of Darbhanga.

The Maithil Brahmins are famous for the orthodoxism and elaborateness in the matters of rites-de-passage and the Pasi living with them must borrow the cultural traits of the dominant caste of the locality.

An All India "Three day Anthropological Conference on the problems of Scheduled castes" was held from November 19 to 21, 1975 Council of Social and Cultural Research, Bihar and Ranchi University Anthropological Association jointly sponsored the Conference. A large number of delegates from India and abroad attended the Conference and contributed papers. Problems of Scheduled castes in Bengal were presented in the conference by P.K. Bhowmick. L.K. Mahapatra talked about the problems of Scheduled castes in orissa. Problems of Scheduled castes of Bihar were highlighted by Dr. L.P. Vidyarthi and Dr. N.Mishra Shri Ram Ratan Ram, the then Minister for Jail and Welfare, Bihar, Dr. A.K. Dhan, the then Vice-Chancellor, Ranchi University, Dr. Fredric Barth of Norway, Dr. R.W. Stevenson of Indo-Canadian Institute, Dr. Vinasheel Gautam, Narayanjee and many other scholars, govt. officials and delegates participated in the three day Conference.

Dr. L.P. Vidyarthi presented a paper "Untouchability in the Republic of India" while introducing the seminar. This paper is full of the problems suffered by the Harijans. The author has very rightly observed that our objective to do good to the Harijans has suffered at three levels of: (1) Policy, (2) Implementation as well, (3) Recruitment and training personel , "At policy level, to my mind, it is an inappropriate approach to lump together the problems of Scheduled castes and scheduled tribes under one Commissioner of Scheduled castes and scheduled tribes... ecologically, demographically, economically and culturally they reflect different situations and hence a correct understanding of the problems and the steps taken for their amelioration deserves two distinct policies, programmes and implementation machinery".

The author has very aptly raised another significant point when he observes that the term Harijan or Scheduled castes has been used as a blanket term to indicate a long list of backward castes; though they suffer from distinct type of social disabilities, economic problems and the like. His classification of the scheduled castes into following group is very scientific :

1. Core groups engaged in scavenging and allied occupation like the Bhangi, the Mehtar, the Hari etc.
2. Communities engaged in leather and allied works like the Chamar and the Ghasi.
3. The Artisan or skilled specialised groups like the Pasi the Turi etc. and
4. The peripherial communities like the Dusadh etc.

Lastly the author has indicated his reaction when he observes that in urban areas certain sections of the Scheduled castes have still to carry buckets of night soil over heads. And to put an end to this system which is not only unhygenic but also indignified and inhuman, he recommends a time-bound programme so that in a limited period of time they become capable of being absorbed in the mainstream of the Indian society.

"Thinking about the problems of Scheduled castes in India" may be regarded as an excellent research paper of L.P. Vidyarthi, presented in Andhra Pradesh State Harijan Conference held at Hyderabad from 10th to 12th April, 1976. The field work data for the paper have been collected from Bihar. Talking about the problems of the Scheduled castes, the author has very emphatically observed: At the very outset, let me make it clear that I am holding the thesis that the problems of the Scheduled castes and the Scheduled tribes are of two different types and deserve to be tackled from different angles". This assertion of the author is very important and useful. Another problem which the author has focussed is that owing to mythological, historical and contextual reasons along with their association with the impure occupations certain stigma in their social relationship has been added, and they have been considered ritually impure by the high caste Hindus, though they enjoyed important functional roles. These have led to different types of social inequality and disability and even today sometimes they are subjected to inhuman atrocities against which they can revolt effectively.

The author has evaluated the welfare measures of the Government which were meagre and made to fail. In this respect also his observations are very useful. He holds the opinion that it is for want of adequate planning and programmes as well as due to change in the attitude of the people in general that the evil effects of untouchability are prolonged and reported profusely from the rural India. Numerious voluntary organisations right from the early days of Mahatma Gandhi to the present time have done their best to eradicate the three fold evils of poverty, exploitation and disabilities from among the so called Harijans. The voluntary organisations are being weakened for want of adequate support. The author is sorry about that.

Thus to sum up the findings of the paper, this could be said the author has thought over the problems of the scheduled castes independently and presented many novel ideas. He has been critical about the failure of the programmes and has given correct and practical suggestions to ameliorate the lot of Scheduled castes.

The year of 1976 was fruitful for the scheduled caste researches because two research scholars Mr. B.M. Mukherjee and Miss Indira Bhattacharya offered to do their Ph.D. researches on the problem of the scheduled castes of Bihar under ths supervision of Dr. N. Mishra of Department of Anthropology, Ranchi University. Whereas Shri Mukherjee chose 'problems of disability among the Scheduled castes', Miss Bhattacharya offered 'the problems of inequality among the Scheduled castes of Bihar'. Both of them have done their field work and it is expected that they will submit their thesis by 1978.

The year of 1977 has been unique for the publication of "Harijan Today" jointly written by L.P. Vidyarthi and N. Mishra, the details of which have been given earlier. It goes without saying that this year also a few M.A. students have offered to write field report's on the problems of the Scheduled castes for which they have already done field works in the villages of Mithila and Bhojpur. Again this year a batch of students went for their field work among the Scheduled castes of Darbhanga. It is expected that a monograph on the Musahar will be published very soon.

Very recently N. Mishra has written a paper "Traditional political organisation of the Dhobis of Darbhanga which has been published in the J.S.S., Vol. XXI 1978 Ranchi. As is evident from the very title, it is a study in the political organisation of a Scheduled caste of Darbhanga in North Bihar where the field work was done. The author has very carefully studied the working of the "Atha-gama Dhobi Jatiya Panchayat'. The nature of crimes, their trail and punishment have been very cautiously depicted in the paper. In the last, the author has mentioned that establishment of state sponsored gram panchayat and construction of a metalled road connecting the villages in question from Darbhanga with a regular bus service proved a fatal jolt for the said caste panchayat. Now the Atha-gama Dhobi Jatiya Panchayat which was so powerful about twenty years ago has practically been defunct and is bound to decay in no time.

Observations

Although the term Scheduled castes and Harijans are of late evolution, they have lived in India even in the early vedic periods. The Hindu scriptures treat them as the 'Chandalas' or the 'patitas' and in censuses they have been called as 'Depressed classes', 'Unclean castes' and 'Exterior castes'. The Govt.of India Act of 1935 declared them as the Scheduled castes and Mahatma Gandhi called them Harijans, Whatever be the term to address then they remained untouchable, unapproachable and indignified suffering from various disabilities and stigma, In the state of Bihar there are 23 Scheduled castes having a population of 8 million. Scheduled caste studies in Bihar have remained shadowed under the tribal studies. In the initial stage Hunter, Dalton, Buchanan, Gait, Risley, O' Melley and Grierson wrote descriptive account either for the census or statistics or for village notes. They were administrators and had no training in doing the field work nor they had idea of research methods. Thus, this phase of the work among the Scheduled castes was done mostly by the foreigners and call this 'Initial stage' for the obvious reasons.

In the second stage there are a few good works particularly those of Briggs, Roy, Hutton, Roy Choudhary and others when they started writing monographs and bit problem oriented papers. This stage I call the 'generating stage'. Then comes the third and the final stage in the history of the students on the Scheduled castes of Bihar. There are perceptible changes both in quality and volumes in this phase. This starts roughly from 1973 from when planned field works. All India Seminars, and research publications of high order among the Scheduled castes were seen. The Post-Graduate Department of Anthropology, Ranchi University under the dynamic leadership of Prof. Vidyarthi deserves thanks for this. Large scale research works, publications of special number on the scheduled castes of Journal of Social Research, organisation of seminars on the problems of the Scheduled castes, writing of M.A. and Ph.D. dissertations on the problems of the Scheduled castes, High quality works of Vidyarthi, Sahay and Mishra particularly the publication of 'Harijan Today' temptated me to declare the third stage as the 'climax' in the Scheduled caste studies, though we have yet to cover a long distance in this regard.

2

SOME ASPECTS OF THE DUSADH OF DARBHANGA

According to the census report of 1981 the scheduled castes constitute 14.51 of the total population of Bihar, the figure for the scheduled tribes comes to 9.05 percent only. But the scheduled tribes have a comparatively high literacy race, i.e. 9.16 percent as against 5.96 percent of the scheduled castes. The members of the scheduled caste are more backward than those of the scheduled tribes. These economically backward and socially incompatible people of our country deserve special attention of the government and of the anthropologists.

Who are the Scheduled Castes

Tracing the origin of the Scheduled Castes one has to go back to the origin of caste itself. According to the classical theory of Varna those who sprang from the mouth of the Brahma (Creator) were called the Brahmins, from the arms were called the Kshatrya, from the thinghs were called the Vaishya and from feet were called the Shudra. The Shudras came out from the lowest part of the body as hence hold the lowest position in the Varna hierarchy. The scheduled castes of today belong to the Shudra Varna. A brief review of the scheduled castes as treated in the decineal censuses may be useful.

In the year 1901 Risley, then Census Commissioner of India attempted for the first time to classify the Hindu castes according to their social standing. Accordingly the population was divided into the following seven categories: 1. Brahmans, 2. Castes other than Brahmans who rank above clean Shudras, 3. Clean Shudras 4. Clean castes served by the degraded Brahmans, 5. Castes other than group 4 whose water is not taken, 6. Unclean castes, 7. Unclean feeder. In the census of 1911, an enquiry was instituted to ascertain the castes and tribes which suffered specified religious and social disabilities. Although the term "Depressed Class" has been mentioned in the Census report of 1921, the Castes constituting the depressed class have not been defined. The term "Depressed Classes" were more elaborately dealt with in the census report of 1931 in which 31 castes were listed. The term "Exterior Castes" was also used for "Depressed Castes" before 1930, but since the enactment of the Government of India Act of 1935 they have been consistently referred to as Scheduled Castes. The many untouchable castes in different parts of India were listed in a separate Schedule in the Act and this practice was continued in the constitution of India 1950. The list of Scheduled Caste can be altered only by the President of India. The word Harijans (Children of Hari or God) which was used by Mahatma Gandhi for the untouchables is almost invariably employed as a synonym for the scheduled caste. In Bihar 24 communities have been declared as Scheduled castes whose population according to the census of 1961 is 65, 36, 875 while as per the census of 1971 out of the total population of Bihar, i.e. 56, 353, 369, they constitute 14.11 percent of the states population.

Importance of Studying Dusadhs

The Dusadhs are the second largest Scheduled caste of Bihar. Their total population is 26,55,832 which is only next to Chamars 29,78,562. But while we have a full length book on the life and culture of Chamars by Geo. W. Briggs (1920) there is none about the Dusadhs. The Dusadhs belong to the weaker section of the population. They are illiterate, landless, defamed, indebted, unemployed exploited, disorganised and un-fed living in the remote villages of North Bihar. Their socio-economic problems are more acute than those of the other members of the Scheduled castes and tribes of Bihar. They are enlisted among the criminal castes. Before undertaking suitable measures for the amelioration of their conditions it is rather necessary to make a general survey of their socio-economic conditions and the factors which make them criminal.

Planning Field work among the Dusadhs of Darbhanga

The district of Darbhanga has been selected for the study of the

Dusadhs as it constitutes the district of the largest concentration of this caste. It is clearly reflected from the following table:

Name of the Dist.	Total Population
Darbhanga	1,13,513
Muzaffarpur	1,36,303
Gaya	1,67,130
Patna	1,73,915

Most of the Dusadhs of Darbhanga district are agricultural labourers. The district has 3009 villages and only 7 small towns; 95.8 percent of its total population live in the villages. Darbhanga is amply suited for studying an agricultural labour community like the Dusadh, for here the impact of urbanisation and industrialisation is extremely negligible.

The field work for this paper was done in a few villages both urban and rural in the district of Darbhanga Machhaita and Mohanpur as rural villages and Choona Bhathi and Laxmi Sagar as urban villages or suburbs of Darbhanga town. The village of Machhaita is situated at a distance of about 30 miles east of Darbhanga town, Mohanpur is about five miles east of Darbhhanga, Choona-Bhathi and Laxmi Sagar are two miles east of Darbhanga. Machhaita was selected for a detailed study for it is the most remote village free from the impact of industrialisation, urbanisation and modernisation; it has maintained the traditional feature of a Caste village. Most of the data on the cultural persistance have been collected from this village; the other villages namely, Choona Bhathi, Laxmi Sagar and Mohanpur, which are nearer to the town, have been selected for evaluating culture change.

Cultural background of the area

The term Darbhanga is a corrupt form of "Dwara Bung" or the gate way of Bengal. It is said that before the development of the modern means of communication, people used to march to Bengal via Darbhanga. Perhaps because of this interaction the Maithils of Darbhanga and the Bengalis share many items of culture in common. Another view is that Darbhanga derived its name from one Darbhangi Khan a very rich famous landlord of this place in distant past.

The district of undivided Darbhanga covers an area of 3,345 square miles extending from 25-28 to 26-40 north latitude and 85.31 to 86.44 east longitude. It is bounded on the north by Nepal; on the south by the Ganga river which separates it from the district of Patna and by the Begusarai district, on the east, by the district of Saharsa and on the west by the Muzaffarpur district.

It appears that the term Tirhut which is a corrupt form of Teer-Bhukta refers to a cultural and linguistic area situated on the banks of the Kamla, the Balan and the Bagmati rivers, which partially covers the district of Darbhanga. It is believed that during the Pauranic period the territory of Darbhanga was extended upto Nepal.

The district of Darbhanga has been a strong hold of Maithil culture, Culturally Mithila stands apart pre-eminently as the land given to intellectual pursuits and consequently to speculations about the spiritual well being of man. It was mostly here, in this land of Mithila, that the great Brahma-vidya was perfected which is the essence of Vedanta and is the kernel round which Hindu culture has developed. We can justly feel proud of the eminent trio Janaka, Yagnavalkya and Gautama. The name of Janaka stands out as a symbol Videha (without a body) for be cared little for the material things. Though living in midst of royal luxuries, he remained un-attached to them. He was regarded as an emblem of perfect wisdom. Great sages like Sukadeva approached him for Brahma Jaana. The Maithils are so orthodox and elaborate in the discharge of their sacred obligations that there is a general law applicable to the entire followers of Hindu Dharma that if and when the Sastrachar (textual rules) regarding a domestic rite is vague or silent the custom of Mithila in that respect should be followed without any delay.

It is in this area of Brahmanic classical culture where we examine the Dusadhs an allegedly criminal caste occupying the lowest rung in the Brahmanic society.

Origin of the Dusadh

In the absence of any authentic written record about the origin of the Dusadh, one has to depend necessarily on the oral tradition. There are several legends regarding the origin of the Dusadh caste:

According to a legend current among some sections of the Dusadhs they are the descendants of the great Kaurava king Dussashan. The Kauravas were responsible for the dreadful war of Mahabharat, and their descendants were cursed become an object of hate and destitude. The Kauravas were of lunar origin (Chandra Bansi) and the Dusadhs also claim to be of Chandra Bansi Kachatrya origin.

Another legend puts the Dusadhs under the caste of the Gahlot Rajputas. This is a very widely known myth which says that during the time of king Shiladitya once Ballimipur the capital city of the then Rajasthan, was attacked by enemy. The king Shiladitya was killed in this war. And as per convention, except queen Puspavati who was then in the family way his several wives burnt themselves alive in order to perform Jauhar or Sati. Puspavati escaped to the Maliya range and got shelter in a cave. After some time a son was born to her. As the boy was born in a Guha (Cave) Later on Goha was called by the names of Gohaditya, Guhil and Guhadhtta. Goha was brought up by Kamlavati (a Brahmin women) as Puspavati the mother of Goha, died. Goha was a very sharp minded boy who managed to get the estate of Idur from the king Mandalik who was by then very old. Mandalik, a Bhil by tribe, was later on killed by Goha. Goha had now a clean sailing. His descendents adopted this name for the gotra of all the members of that bansha (root). This practice continued till the year 1257 A.D. when Rahup a Gahlout managed to regain, his ancestoral kingdom of Chitour from the king of Kalour.There were two main changes during his regime. The first was the adoption Sisodiya gotra as a substitute for the Gahilot and the second was the change in the title from Rahup to Rana. Again roughly after two hundred years in the year 1439 when Rana Lakha was crowned there were sporadic risings of the Mughal in various places of the Eastern India. It is interesting to note that the sacred city of Gaya was also attacked by the Mughals and Rana Lakha (Lax Singh) had brought an army of selected brave Rajputas to purge out the enemy from the sacred soil of Gaya. Rana Lakha was killed in the battle field at Gaya while chasing the enemy. It is believed that the town of Lakhisarai (old name Lakhi Dera) in the district of Monghyr was then founded to commemorate the yoman's service of Lakha Singh. After the death of Lakha Singh there was some confusion in his army organisation. A section of his army preferred to stay in Bihar to protect the Hindu sacred against Muslim invasion whereas others were forced to stay in this very geographical area as their retreat to Rajasthan was not possible due to communicational problems. Hence this race of Sisodiya Rajput settled in and around Gaya, and in course of time they migrated to other parts of Bihar. The original Gahlot branched off into the following 24 branches: 1. Ahriya, 2. Mangolia, 3. Sisodiya, 4. Pipra, 5. Kailaya, 6. Guhner, 7. Chorniaya, 8. Godab, 9. Majropa, 10. Bhimla, 11. Kankot, 12. Kotecha 13. Sora, 14. Uhar, 15. Useba, 16. Nirup, 17. Nadodya, 18. Nadhota, 19. Bhojkara, 20. Kuchera, 21. Dusadh, 22. Bhetbara, 23. Paha and 24. Purot. Of these many branches of the Gahlots are no longer found anywhere.

Dusadhs and their Divisions

Dusadhs are sub-divided into the following eleven sub-branches 1. Maghaiya, 2. Kamur, 3. Paliwar, 4. Baburchi, 5. Kurin, 6. Silontha, 7. Surjha, 8. Kanoujia, 9. Bahelia, 10. Madeshiya, 11. Dharhi. In the village Machhaita only Maghaiya Dusadhs are found, in Laxmisagar and Chuna Bhathi there are few families of Kurin but there majority of the Dusadhs are of the Maghaiya branch. All the eleven branches of Dusadh now function as independent and endogamous sub-castes.

As has been mentioned earlier, the bench line data for this paper are drawn from Machhaita, a brief description of various ethnic groups of this village is given below:

SI.	Name of the Caste	No. of Families	Total population
1.	Brahmin	134	521
2.	Dusadh	35	322
3.	Kebat	5	26
4.	Chamar	5	22
5	Teli	2	14
6.	Hazam	1	8
7.	Barhi	1	6
		183	829

The settlement pattern of the village is composed of five hamlets or tolas. Two tolas are occupied by the Brahmins one exclusively by the families of ex-landlords locally known as Daudhi and the other is called Babhan toli where the commoners among the Brahmans live. The other three tolas are named after the numerically dominant caste, such as Dusadh toli, Kebat toli and Chamar toli. This is a general pattern of Hindu caste. The Harijans are almost invariably settled on the outskirt of the main village formed by the upper castes and the clean shudras.

The position of the Dusadh in the Caste hierarchy

It has been mentioned earlier that the Dusadhs belong to Shudra Varna, but among the Shudra also there is a hierarchy of position. However, the position of each of the castes or jatis within a Varna is not clearly marked even in the Manu Smriti which is an authentic scripture dealing such matters. In practice the hierarchy of position is generally vague and complex. While varna hierarchy is clearly borne out, the various jatis within a varna are sometimes distinguished by the tradition of food and water. For instance, the Dusadhs do not drink water touched by Chamars, Mehtars, Doms, Halalkhors and Dhobis whereas the latter may accept water from the hands of Dusadh. A Dusadh will accept food and water from a Pasi whereas the latter will not accept water from a Dusadh. Sometimes this position is challenged by the castes treated inferior. Yet, traditionally, the Dusadh is inferior to the Pasi, on par with the Musahar and superior to the Chamar, the Mehatar, the Dom, the Dhobi and the Halalkhore of the area under study.

To know the reasons that make the Harijan untouchable the answers given by the Brahmin informants may be classified in the following groups:

1. Those who follow unclean occupation
2. Those who keep pigs or eat beef or pork
3. Those who wander about and have no settled home to return

Untouchability and the Dusadh

Despite the fact that in the constitution of India the practice of untouchability has been made an offence by the untouchability offence

Act, of 1955, the Dusadhs are still discriminated against in the matter of social intercourse. They are not allowed to take water from the well used by the upper castes. However, in each village there is a well, popularly known as the Barovarna well which be used by the socalled low-castes. Similarly in the pond, which is used for bathing and washing dirty clothes, the Dusadhs are not allowed to use the ghat where the Brahmins take bath or wash their clothes; the former may have a separate ghat. The Dusadhs are denied entry to the temple where Brahmins are the priest; exception to this rule is made in the case of Shiva temple. Their caste deity, called Salhesh, is enshrined generally under a banyan tree. Also they have no entry to the house of a clean caste. As they are landless labourers they have to go to take boiena (wage in grains) from the employers, but in the house of their clean caste master they are kept off, never allowed to be under the roof of the house. This treatment is supported by two reasons firstly, they are unclean and hence they will pollute the house and all the articles kept there in and secondly, one is afraid that if they come to see anything during the day they may steal it at night.

Social history of the Dusadh

The Dusadhs have eleven sub-castes and two common titles Paswan and Das. Paswan is the most common title whereas Das has certain status value. Das is normally affixed with the names of such persons who are either Kabir Panthi or Ojha Gunee, or otherwise elevated from the commoners. In the urban areas sometimes they have found using such titles as Prasad and Singh. A Dasach informant very proudly explained me that the very meaning of the term Dusadh is the one difficult to be controlled and the Paswan title also refers to heroic deeds the protector or a strong watchman.

The social history of the Dusadh is the history of oppression, exploitation, met with over centuries. It is said that during the Mughal rule the Dusadhs were tortured and their young women were raped and kidnapped by the Muslims. To protect the chastity of their women they adopted two protective measures firstly they gave their daughters in marriage at an early age, even before five years and secondly, they started rearing pigs on large scale so that they could chase the Muslims with the help of pigs (at the very sight of the pigs the Muslims would run away). Further more, as a protective measure, the Dusadhs began eating pork, and their unmarried girl is required to put on a small piece of the bone of a pig in the form of a tabij round her neck. The Dusadh informants held that they are the descendants of the Gahlot Rajputs, and hence their girls are more fair in complexion than those of any other Harijan community, but this beauty was a curse for them during the Moughal period. To make their beautiful girls ugly, so as to save them from the cruel hands of the rapacious Muslims they started tattoing (Godna) on most of the exposed parts of their body.

Marriage

The Dusadhs have eleven endogamous sub-divisions, marriage outside one's sub-caste is not tolerated, nor marriage with any "blood relation" is practised. They prefer village exogamy, but in urban areas one may marry in the same Mohalla. They practise child marriage. The girl's father is very anxious to settle the marriage of his daughter for the following reasons :

(a) There is a dearth of boys among the Dusadh. The females out number males in as much as there were 1,42,587 females against 1,31,436 males among the Dusadhs of Darbhanga in the year 1961.

(b) Poor economic condition of the Dusadh is another limiting factor for an early marriage. The bride's father has to manage for five pieces of clothes (pancha took kapra) and a crown (mor) for the groom in addition to the expenses on the feast and rituals.

(c) Early marriage is supposedly helpful in cheeking premarital sex relations.

(d) To keep grown up daughter unmarried is the greatest disgrace for the Dusadh society.

The striking feature in the Dusadh's negotiation for marriage is the consideration of the physical suitability of the couple. Being illiterate, they generally ascertain the age of the couple in terms of height. Before leaving for the groom's house the bride's father measures the height of his daughter with a bamboo stick (penga or pharathi). On reaching the groom's house he takes the measurement of the height of the groom with the penga. If the groom is shorter than the bride the settlement is ruled out. If the bride and the groom are of the same stature, the contracting parties give due consideration to the issue. Generally, the groom is preferred to be taller than the bride. After setting the consent of the groom's parents and fixing a date for the ghardekki (inspection of the groom's house) the father of the bride comes back home. On the date fixed for ghardekhi the father of the bride generally with five friends and relations again goes to the groom. When they reach at the groom's house, the party is received by the father of the groom. No sooner they are seated on a patia made of mothi (mat) they are served with hukka pani. The father of groom may also invite a few friends and relations for a baiski (sitting on hukka and bidi tamaku). The marriage is settled after the terms and conditions are acceptable to both the parties. Usually five pieces of clothes and some quantity of rice are demanded by the groom's father. The main issue in bargaining is the number of barat. The bride's father shows his inability to feed a large barat party while groom's father insists on inviting a large number, and finally there is a compromise between the two. An auspicious date for the marriage is fixed, generally between March and April when they are free from agricultural activities.

On the date of marriage the barat party proceeds either on foot or in some cases in bullock cart. Led by musicians playing dhol pipahi, the barat proceeds to the bride's house. On the way, if there is a toddy-shop the members of the barat party stop to have, at least, one lavani (a local earthen pot of toddy). The groom wears a distinct ceremonial dress called the jora jama of pink colour and a mor the head gear. When the barat party reaches the house of the bride some elderly persons come ahead to receive it. The guests are offered gurpani and hukka chilam follows soon. The marriage rites are few and brief. No Brahmin is called to officiate at the ceremony, and the barber does the ritual of lahchho. Lahchho is a ritual in which a few drops of blood from the little finger of the bride's left hand is taken out and the groom chew betels containing the blood. Similarly a few drops of blood from the little of the groom's right hand is taken for the bride. The barat is fed rice, pulse and a few vegetables. In some cases curd and sugar may also be served. Next day when the barat party is getting ready for going back, coloured water is sprinkled on the clothes of the guests.

Widow re-marriage is very common. Divorce is also allowed. But in the case of re-marriage of the widow there is practically no ceremonial formalities. Since that stature is the only consideration for the suitability of the mates and not the age, it quite often happens that the bride is older than the groom. Generally, the marriage is solemnized when the couple is in infancy. Later on, in some cases the bride attains maturity while the groom is still a boy. Consequently, particularly in the urban areas, such married girls often pick up boy friends.

Normally in case of a virgin marriage there is a gap of ten to fifteen years between marriage and the second marriage (gauna) after which consumation takes place. Before that the groom seldom visits his wife and hence even after marriage the couple fails to meet their sexual urge, and very often they develop extramarital sexual intimacy. In such cases, after gauna, the girl often runs away from her husband's house and suffers from hysteric of what is known as bhutlaggi (possession of devil spirit). Sometimes the groom may turn up dwarf while the bride becomes tall; when the groom's father comes to finalise the date of the gauna he is sore at the disparity in the stature of the couple. In such cases there may be difficulty in materialising the gauna ceremony; even if it works the bride may run away from her husband's house, as she becomes a laughing stock there. Since the rate of infant mortality is very high among the Dusadhs, one of the spouse may die, and this also necessitates remarriage.

Conception

When the girl finds that her menstruation flow has ceased for consecutive two three months she discloses her pregnancy. The village Chamain (wife of a Chamar) is consulted for the confirmation of pregnancy who conveys it in a very guarded language (so and so is heavy) to the mother or the mother-in-law of the expectant mother. Then the elderly persons of the family come to know about this. The pregnant girl is treated softly within the limited means. She is not allowed to carry a heavy load as it might cause an abortion. Going out during the early morning or late evening is also avoided due to various magico religious belief. She is called Dujiba (or two souls in one body) during the period of her pregnancy. Dujiba deserves special attention not only by the members of her own family but also by all the persons. Particularly, females of the village regardless of caste and kin. Some ladies may serve her cooked vegetables and pulse and sometime rice. The gift of this sort is always a welcome rendering a moral support not only to the expectant mother but also to the entire family. During the first pregnancy, an expectant mothers likes to be with her own parents when she expects more comforts and care. No ritual is performed at the birth of the child.

Death Rites

Marriage and death are the two occasions when one has to feed some castemen. The death pollution is observed for one month. Dead children are burried; and in case of adult, if fuel can be managed, the deceased is creamated or is thrown into the river Balan after inducing fire in the month of the dead which is locally known as mukhagni or uk-jharkayab. No Brahmin is called, Sometimes a degraded Brahmin meant for the Harijans may be called, who would not accept food and water but sidha and cash dakshina are given. In urban area a dusadh declares himself to be the priest performing the act of a Brahman.

Economic Life

Economically the Dusadhs are very backward. As has been mentioned earlier they are landless in true sense because even their homestead belongs to some landlords. In Darbhanga district the landlords usually settle some labours on their land to assure the regular supply of labour during transplantation and harvest. It is a peculiar type of Jajmani system in which payment has to be done for each deal, but the labours have to serve the ex-landlord. In case of difference with the owner of the land, a Dusadh may be compelled to leave the place.

There is practically no industry in the whole of Darbhanga district, excepting a few sugar factories which provide seasonal employment.

The entire labourer community has to fall back upon agriculture. The Dusadhas are agricultural labourers. Depending on the requirements of the agricultural activities, the Dusadhs are in demand only for four months and the rest of the year they are either fully or partially unemployed. Even during the busy period of agricultural operations and particularly for the transplantation which is supposed to be tiring for hard labour the employer has the following preferences. A labourer should be; (i) a male of age group between 20 to 40 years, (ii) must not be dull, (iii) may work to complete the transplantation work even off the time (on some nominal payment) and (iv) must not indulge in gossip. There is no demand for female and young boys of 16-19. In the circumstances, in a nuclear family there will be roughly only one man who has some job opportunity. Regarding the payment of the wage, which is always in kind, one gets $2\frac{1}{2}$ seers of paddy or 2 seers of marua or wheat for the day's work.

During winter harvest, job opportunity increases considerably. Since the paddy field has to be harvested in a day, even children and women are engaged for this purpose. The payment is made in accordance with the number of bundles harvested and carried to khalihan (thrashing floor). Normally a labourer gets one bundle for every sixteen bundles harvested and carried to khalihan of the employer agriculturist. This is the only season for the Dusadhs when all of them get jobs and when they can collect some paddy after working hard from dawn to dusk. A Dusadh family can save some paddy to pay off the debt and also for future hard months of enemployment.

Thus, scarce job opportunity and hardships compel the Dusadhs to go for seasonal migration to Nepal, Bhutan, Calcutta, Assam and the jute producing area of the district of Purnea where they have good job opportunity at a satisfactory wage. Normally, they visit these places after the paddy transplantation is over and come back by the time of winter harvest. But this seasonal migration is also limited to young men alone. There are some very serious drawbacks of this migration. Most of the Dusadhs fall ill due to inhospitable climatic condition of the places rainy season. Sometimes their entire saving is stolen away while they are out at work. The cases of fraud and of pickpocket at the time of return journey to village home are also very high. It is because of such incidence that the saying goes "Calcutta Kamai Calcutta gamai" the earning obtained in Calcutta is spent in Calcutta.

Some Dusadhs who are settled on the lands of a landlord, get land for share cropping, but they have to serve the master frequently as begar (on some nominal tips). As has been mentioned earlier, the earning of a common Dusadh family is very low; hence even to maintain the family is a Herculus task for them. Most of the Dusadh children prefer to serve as cow boys in the families of the landlords to evade starvation.

The Dusadhs live in a small hut made of bamboo and dry grasses. The building materials are very scarce in north Bihar. Only a few persons in the village have bamboo grooves and timber. The Dusadhs are compelled either to beg or to steal the building materials. Similarly, there is a scarcity of fuel. Domestic coal is very costly and the firewood is meant only for those who have either some big mango orchard or can purchase it at a high price. The poor Dusadhs have to depend on the landlords who own orchard for obtaining fuel. They sometimes stealthly cut green branches of mango trees and then fetch them after a few days when they dry up. For this they often get good beatings.

Thus, the Dusadhs live in abject poverty, have no job opportunity and are forced to lead a miserable life. The circumstances are such that they have to choose between stealing and starvation, and they do prefer to be thieves than to die unnatural death.

Political Organisation

The Dusadhs of village Machhaita have a caste panchayat which is headed by Tilesi Das known as the Manjyan. The post of Manjyan is hereditary. In order to rank next to him is Chharidar who is nominated by the Manjyan and whose duty is that of a messanger. For important caste matters, like divorce or irregular sexual union, the decision of the caste panchayat is final. But the peculiarity of the Dusadh caste panchayat of Machhaita is that for the trial of a case they approach the local landlords and hence this caste panchayat is a puppet in the hands of the landlords. With the introduction of the new Gram Panchayat the Dusadh Jati Panchayat is rather defunct. Now all the cases are tried by the Gram Panchayat. The failure of the traditional caste panchayat of the Dusadhs seems to be on account of their being landless and consequently dependent upon the landlords for the whole of their life personal needs and authority.

Religious Life

In addition to all the gods and deities worshipped by the Brahmins of the village, the Dusadhs have a separate set of divinity headed by Salhesh Maharaj or Rajaji Salhesh is the supreme deity of the Dusadhs. In Machhaita, there is a small temple of Salhesh made of thatched roof in a corner of the village. There are four terracotta images of males and one of female in the temple. Rajaji is seated on an elephant, three other images are those of Chuharmal a famous wrestler and the military secretary of Salhesh; the third image is that of Moti-Ram who is said to be his brother, and the forth image is of Karikant who is his nephew (sister's son), and these two fellows are his body guards. The solitary female image is of Dauna-Malin who loved Salhesh Maharaj. The Dusachs believe that Salhesh had his ancestoral home in Phulbari near Biratnagar a district of Nepal where there is a very old temple of Salhesh which is a place of pilgrimage for the Dusadhs of India, and also of those who live in the teraie region of Nepal. In Machhaita, Salhesh Maharaj and his associates Chuhar Mal, Moti Ram, Kari-Kant and Dauna Malin are worshipped regularly by Bhola Paswan who is the Bhagat of Salhesh. Salhesh is a vegetarian deity hence, no animal is sacrificed. He likes laddo and pan and also milk puddings. Once in a year the Dusadhs celebrate Salheshpuja at the village level, generally in the month of Baisakh or Shravan, when they collect bher (subscriptions) from all the Dusadh families. The Brahmins also offer bher generously. Salhesh is worshipped ceremoniously with great excitement and pomp. Salhesh is believed to be possessed with divine strength and is capable of granting good health and sufficient strength to his devotees. The landless agricultural labourers count upon their health alone, and hence the Dusadh's veneration to Salhesh as their supreme deity is but natural.

In addition to Salhesh they worship Bhuinya, Sokha and Gainya at the family level. These are believed to be spirits who if appeased, may bring prosperity in life. They also worship Rahu occasionally but as this worship involves considerable amount of money, in Machhaita, Rahu puja was performed only some twenty years ago. On the occasion of Rahu Puja the Bhagat walks bare footed on the burning fire, dips his hand in boiling milk and also walks on the sharp edge of a sword without having any injury. They have respect for the gods and goddesses of the Brahmins, but have no entry to the Brahmanic temples. They bow their heads before these inaccessable gods from a distance. However, some temples of Shiva are open to them. The Dusadhs restrain themselves from entering Brahmanic temples, generally being afraid of violating the norms and pollutting the temple. They celebrate only a few festivals on a mini scale. The belief in witch craft and Bhoot Pret is looked after by the Bhagats and Baithki.

Dusadhs--a Criminal Caste

It has been mentioned earlier that the very caste of the Dusadh is defamed as being criminals. In certain villages there is a heavy concentration of criminal Dusadhs; in the district of Darbhanga, Chhachha, Mohanpur, Balia, Raima, Kothia, Belmohan and Babubarhi villages are notorious for sheltering expert thieves.

The Dusadhs are not the only criminal caste; there are a large number of criminal tribes in various parts of Northern India like the Bhat, the Sansi, the Karwal, the Habura, the Tagu, the Pakhwara, the Mina, the Bawari, the Hami and many others. It is alleged that the members of a criminal caste or a tribe have taken up crime as their hereditary profession and means of livelihood. But nobody seems to bother the question as to how and why one resorts to criminal practices, what are the compelling factors responsible for inducing one to susk disgraceful act. Why should one lead a degraded, defamed and disgraceful life, full of scorns, hatred and regret at the risk of life, if a respectful life full of peace and prestige can be possible. In the following pages we shall make attempt to examine these questions with special reference to the Dusadhs of Darbhanga district.

As has been mentioned earlier, the Dusadhs are by the large landless people having no traditional occupation of their own, consequently they do not figure anywhere in the network of the Jajmani system. However, they claim that they are the descendants of the Gahlout Rajput, suggesting thereby that they are brave, enterprising and gallant. They say that their title of the Pasman is a corrupt of Paswan which means a watchman, a guard (The British Government had also appointed Dusadhs as village watchmen an occupation which in most cases the later followed hereditarily). In support of their claim, as has been noted earlier, they hold that they migrated from Rajasthan to Gaya then to Lakhisarai and finally from there to Darbhanga. Their claim is however totally ignored by the other castes who treat them as Shudras and not the Rajputs. This has obviously lead them to develop antagonism towards the Hindu society in general and affluent landlords in particular. Poverty and social incompatibility thus seem to be the immediate environmental factors responsible for leading the Dusadhs to criminal acts.

The Dusadhs are knwon to be specialists in theft by Singhmari (cutting through a manhole in the outer wall of the house near the foundation) method. A less talented Dusadh, it is said, might be a cattle lifter also. In recent past, some of them have been indulging in dacoity in gang. The thieves of Chhachha had affiliation with the criminals of Nepal. In the Indo Nepal border areas, locally known as the Payakat, these criminals operate as international gang of thieves. Usually they commit theft or robbery in an Indian village and cross the border overnight. This is posing a baffling challenge to Indian police and administration. Of late they have acquired huge arms and ammunition from their partners in Nepal.

In the year 1968 there was a planned attack on the Dusadhs of village of Belmohan. The residents of about twenty five villages around Belmohan, who were in constant threat posed by the criminals of Belmohan, hatched a joint plan to uproot all the 71 families of the Dusadhs of Belmohan. Accordingly one dark night a few thousand irritated villagers attacked the Dusadhs, demolished their houses and ploughed the land on which stood their Kachcha houses (of course, the Dusadhs resettled in this village after sometime). The criminals of this village operated from Silliguri (West Bengal) in the east to Gorakhapur (U.P.) in the west and therefore had attracted the attention of the Police administration of Bihar. In the following pages case history of how the Police administration met the challenge of this menace is recorded to show that even hardened criminals can turn into good citizens if they are dealt with care and sympathy and not the way the above mentioned villagers chose to adopt.

Changing the heart of criminals: an experiment

The Sarvodaya leader Sri Jaiprakash Narayan had launched a welfare Scheme according to which the notorious criminals of the Chambal Valley surrendered before him on the assurance that they will be accepted in society as respectable persons after their voluntary surrender in mass. These criminals took a vow not to commit any crime in future. Some of them were rehabilitated in M.P. This new approach to criminals was welcomed by many people, including those in the administration when Sri Kedar Pandey took as the Chief Minister of Bihar he instructed the police officials to control the crime by all means. A special anticrime drive was launched during the summer of 1972 Sri Shashi Bhushan Sahay, the then D.I.G. Northern Range, and Sri Y.N. Srivastava, the then S.P. of Darbhanga, took the lead in meeting this challenge.

Mr. Shrivastava went to some villages of criminals in Madhubani sub-division in the middle of June 1972, and acquainted himself with the economic and social condition of the criminals. He found that none of them had foodgrains beyond one day's meal and that out of about 4,000 criminals in the district only five were educated. It may be mentioned that long before independence the Dusadhs came under the purview of the Criminal Tribes Act and were subjected to strict surveillance by Police to whom they were legally bound to report under Section 20 of the Act. The C.T. Act was repeated in 1953. As Mr. Shrivastava reports, "the persistent socio-economic exploitation and social hatred life the Dusadhs with no alternative but to indulge in crimes with impunity to eke out their existence. The entire lot of them and habitual law breakers posing a constant threat to the society and peace and order. They had old connections with their Jhijha counter parts in Nepal Tarai and carried depredations in Madhubani and other sub-divisions of Darbhanga district. Although pioneering efforts were first made in 1936 to reclaim these hereditary criminals by the then S.P. Darbhanga, Mr. B.N. Mullick, and to absorb them in the society a positive breakthrough could not be possible. These people had no other occupation, as such fresh blood continued to take over from their elders and thus the nefarious trade passed on from generation to generation. The Dusadhs of village Raiyam it may be recalled, with an unbroken record of carrying their depredations from last one hundred and fifty years, have been constant source of headache to the police administration besides perpetual terror to the rural folk of the region. "The actual life situation of the Dusadhs gave Mr. Srivastava a clue to crime and criminality. He was convinced then that they needed sympathetic consideration. The surrender of Chambal valley criminal was the current example of the day. He did not lose much time. He made written appeals to Raiyam criminals fully assuring them of police help. Social workers of the area also helped the police to win their confidence".

There was a felt need of better and free life among the criminals also. They were tired of the life of criminals. There were lot of torture and humiliation in Hajat and also in Jail. These people had been suffering deprivation and humiliation as outlaws, and their sons and daughters were looked down upon by the society and none was ready to employ them even as menials. All these had been a continuous source of mental agony. After the offer came from the Government to surrender for a happy life, they sat together to discuss the offer and decided in favour of mass surrender before the Govt. the decision was communicated to Mr. Srivastava.

On the evening of June 14,1972 when Mr. Srivastava accompanied by a number of high officials including Mr. K.B. Kumar, A.S.P. Darbhanga and Mr. P. Sinha, S.D.O. Madhubani, reached Raiyam, none of the criminals left the village. Instead all of them along with their family members and children came forward in a procession with unique enthusiasm before the visiting officials. They garlanded the officers and formally surrendered before them. Thereafter, the S.P. along with other officials visited each and house of the criminals and assured them solving their economic problems. The visiting party also distributed sweets among the criminals and their family members.

On the morning of June 15, 1972 the criminals assembled at a well attended public meeting organised in the village and took solemn vow in the name of God not to commit any crime and to lead a "clean life". All together 665 criminals surrenered that, Mr. Shrivastava also addressed the meeting and in order to help them he announced that one member from each criminal family would be taken in Govt. Service. The S.D.O. assured that hard manual schemes would be taken up in the village to provide them jobs.

Just after one month of the 15th of July 72 an impressive function was held at Watson High School in Madhubani. The then Chief Minister of Bihar, Shri Kedar Pandey, and Sri Robi Roy, then I.G. of Police were the Chief guests of the function. One thousand and eight professional criminals of Darbhanga formally surrendered them-selves before the Chief Minister and pledged to lead a normal life as a law abiding citizens. Nineteen gang leaders belonging to different area of Darbhanga district came to the dais one by one, touched the holy Gita, surrendered their arms, and took the vow to abjure the life of a criminal. They took off their turbans placed them at the feet of the Chief Minister who in turn put them again on their heads. The gang leaders were introduced to I.G. by Mr. Shrivastava who gave them the copies of the Gita and the Ramayan.

The portraits of Lord Budha, Mahatma Gandhi, and Acharya Vinoba Bhave formed the back drop of the dais. Prominent citizens of the town, legislators and officials and about 5,000 dependents of criminals watched the solemn function which marked the beginning of a new life by the professional criminals. These outlaws were the old inhabitants of Madhubani sub-division.They mostly belonged to some condemned villages Raiyam and Rajanpura under Jhanjharpur, P.S. Bounsi, Mohanpur, Beldawa, Khajauli, Bapu-Barbi and Belmohan in Phulparas and Loham under Biraul P.S. About a dozen country made guns and pistols, besides live cartridges and house breaking implements used in burglary, were also surrendered. A few criminals surrendered explosives and the chemicals used in manufacturing bombs.

Makardhwaj Paswan, who had participated in about 20 dacoities and over two thousand thefts and burglaries was the first to surrender. He was followed by Ram Bahadur Paswan who had participated in 60 dacoities and had been to jail about a dozen times. Similarly, Jangilal Paswan, Dalsisgar Paswan, Kamla Paswan, Jangi Paswan and Ram Ayodhya Paswan having considerable experiences of theft and dacoity, were recognised terrors of the area. The Chief Minister, Sri Kedar Pande, described the event as momentous and agreed with the I.G. of Police, Mr. Roy, that they should be economically and socially rehabilated if the menace had to be struck at the root.

Amidst thunderous applause the Chief Minister announced immediate financial assistance of Rs. 100/- to each of them. In addition to this all the 550 families which surrendered were promised to be paid Rs. 500/- each for their rehabilitation Mr. Pande lost no time in asuring them priority in Govt. employment and said that 18 of the gang leaders had already been absorbed in Police service and commitment had been made to 40 others.

The I. G. of police Mr. R. Roy said that schools would be opened for the children of the criminals who had surrendered and their families would not be harassed. As to criminals facing prosecution the Police would ensure their trial soon.

The Chief Minister's appeal had a spontaneous and favourable response. The then Co-operation Minister Dr. Jagannath Mishra, Radhanandan Jha, then State Minister for Jail, and a few legislators of the area also announced to donate their one month's salary to the criminals' welfare fund. Mr.Ramphal Paswan M.L.A. announced a donation of Rs. 600/- Madhubani citizens Association announced a donation of Rs. 1001/-. The Mahila Clubs of Madhubani, Laheriasarai and Darbhanga had donated 450 packets of cloths for the criminals, each containing one dhoti, sari and four sets of cloths for children. This was a unique experiment with solving the problems of criminals "changing their heart", it was called.

Confessions

The Dusadhs kept the information regarding their crime confidential among the members of the secret group alone. But after their mass surrender they were frank enough to reveal the criminal acts of past life. The following confessions made by few criminals will reveal as to what motivated them for the crime:

1. **Ramchandra Paswan:** "I belong to village Tenua under Madhubani subdivision! I was born in August 1947 in a poor family of a Dusadh. I was forced to become a criminal to earn one square meal a day. I have not been happy with this life and therefore I have been making concrete efforts to abjure the condemned life. I have passed the B.L. examination and at present I am a post-graduate student at C.M. college, Darbhanga. This year I have appeared also at the State Public Service Commission Examination and have done well. Had there been any positive effort to end socio-economic exploitations of the Dusadh community I would not have been driven to antisocial activities. I remember how the police harassed me and my family members on several occasions unnecessarily for the one or another crime committed by someone else. More than once some of my relatives were out in the hajat and tortured to make confession for the crime which they had not done at all.

   I have tried to build my career, but it is still to be seen whether the society accepts me with open arms and helps me to lead peaceful life of a law abiding people".

2. **Dalsingar Paswan:** "I belong to Tenua under Madhubani sub-division I had been to jail more than 40 times, between 1951 to 1971 for dacoities and hundreds of thefts. I have a country made pistol which I purchased from a blacksmith in Monghyr for Rs. 200/-. I never bothered for the cartridges.They were available in plenty from our sources in the police organisation for a few chips.

   "I am tired of leading the life of a criminal. I have come out of jail in April last only and have decided to surrender for a good future of my sons and daughters. I am grateful to Mr. Y.N. Srivastava, S.P. Darbhanga, who unlike other police officers gave me a shock treatment and inducted me to the fold of law abiding citizens".

3. **Daya Ram Paswan:** "I have passed the I.A. Examination from Bihar University but could not get a job because I belong to the condemned Dusadh community of Raiyam. I have committed no crimes in the eyes of law but yet I am treated like a criminal. I expect a better treatment by the Police and the society".

4. **Ghina Paswan:** "I am from Adarpura. I have been a gang leader and have participated in over 60 dacoities and over 2,000 thefts. When I was only 16 years old, the police put me in a lockup, beat me mercilessly and kept me without food for three days for no fault of mine. In the police lockup itself I took a vow to take a revenge on the police and the society which was responsible for torturing me, ransacking my house and insulting my widow Bhabhi and sister. I have led the life of a criminal for nearly 35 years, but have not gained anything except a bad name. I hope the society will forget my past sins and will accept my children with open arms after I have surrendered with a vow not to repeat the sinful act again".

Observations

1. There has been practically no research on the scheduled castes of Bihar in general and the Dusadhs in particular.
2. In the constitution of India the Scheduled Castes have been tagged with the scheduled tribes, although the scheduled castes have different set of problems and have very little in common, with the scheduled tribes. This fact has to be borne in mind while the Government looks into their problems.
3. There has been Sanskritisation and Rajputisation among the Dusadhs of Darbhanga district. They have adopted many Brahmanic rites and ceremonies viz. the performance to tarpan during the pitrapaksha and the observance of Shama chakeba

festival etc. They claim to be the descendants of Gahlaut Rajputs, and some of them use the title of Prasad in place of Paswan-their traditional caste title. Their appearance, nature, temperament and myth may have something common with the Rajputs, but their claim for a higher caste status has not yet been settled.

4. The Dusadhs have been defamed criminals for more than hundred and fifty years. Socio-economic factors seem to be responsible for the Duşadh's criminality. Besides poverty, exploitation, and social injustice, the high handedness of the Police in the past have also been a contributing factor.

5. The police administration in Bihar deserves congratulation and praise for the anticrime campaign in general and the mass surrender by the Dusadhs of Darbhanga in particular. This phenomenon of surrender has been described as a change of heart, whereby one gives up the way of life of a criminal to which he was forced to lead by circumstances.

However, the surrender itself will not solve the problem. Obviously those who are involved in dacoity, loot and murder cases will have to be tried according to the law of the land. The immediate problem is of the rehabilitation of their wives and children. The Govt. and society must provide them with jobs. The children, if possible, should be segregated from the surroundings in which they had been living so far. With the help of police official they can be sent to reformatory schools. The real problem, however, is of the acceptance of members of the criminal colony by the society. Even after their surrender and taking a vow not to commit any crime, if the society does not absorb them, they may go back to their old trade once again. It is for the police administration to decide as to how it will be tackling the question of rehabilitation. But in my opinion, to scatter them in many villages will help not only to end their ignominy but may also lead to their gradual absorption in society.

3

TRADITIONAL POLITICAL ORGANISATION OF THE DHOBIS OF DARBHANGA

The Dhobi is one of the few ancient castes in India. Reference of this caste are found in the early writings of the Ramayan and the Mahabharata. Lord Rama had banished Sita on a complaint of a Dhobi. Similarly Soma, one whose name the ladies of Mithila observe the Somavari Vrata was also a Dhobin (washer woman). The fact that first Sohag (blessing for the long life of the husband) is offered by the Dhobin in the Maithil marriage, goes to prove that this caste has a legendry origin and is taken auspicious ordinarily and even at the time of Yatra (departure). Dhoba, Safi and Rajak are the synonyms of the Dhobis.

As per census of 1981 numerically this is the fifth largest scheduled caste having a total population of 553380 persons 281559 males and 271821 females for the whole of Bihar. In the census of 1961 their total population for Bihar was 332,245 which was 5.08 percent of the total population of the scheduled castes. In the district of Darbhanga in 1961 they were 29,374 out of which 13,864 were males and 15,510 females. The old district of Darbhanga covers an area of 3,345 squire miles extending from 25°28' to 26°40 N, latitude and 85°44 E longitude. It is bounded on the North by Nepal, on the South by the Ganga river, on the East by the district of Saharsa and on the west by the Mazaffarpur district. Previously Darbhanga was part of the Tirhut Division of North Bihar but presently it is a division itself. Culturally it is the core of the Maithil culture.

Location of the Field

The Dhobis are sporadically distributed in every part of the district and as it is a band of landless people, having specialisation in washing. It is difficult to find their heavy concentration in the villages Functional Caste as they are, they prefer to remain in a particular cluster of the villages to the best utilisation of their services. They have a strong faith in the Jajmani system. Thus, if they fail to get sufficient clients to maintain them, they will starve. This is why that commonly the villages of Darbhanga possess at least 1 to 7 families of Dhobi with the population ranging from about 4 to 35 (see table 1). Thus, for the obvious reasons four villages namely, Kurson, Dadpatti, Dhamuar and Pohaddi, having Dhobi population, were selected for the field work.These villages are in the Sadar sub-division of the Darbhanga district and are within Manigachhi block and police station which is about 30 miles to the south east of the town of Darbhanga. These villages are about two to four miles far from each other but well within the radius of five miles. Excepting Dhamuar which has considerable Muslim population other villages mentioned above are dominated by the Brahman.The Dusadh, the Musahar, the Sonar, the Kebat, the Kujara, the Dom and the Chamar are the other castes living in these villages. Agriculture is the main source of livelihood of the people of this area. Thus barring a few artisan communities like the Barhi, the Teli, Potter, the Doms, the Sonars and the like others are either agriculturists or agricultural labours.

Social Standing

India is notoriously famous for multiplicity of castes some of which are clean while other unclean. Among the unclean also there is hierarchy. It is very difficult to determine definitely the actual position of a particular untouchable caste as there as multiplicity in the theories regarding the evaluation of their hierarchy. While according to one theory the hierarchy is established on the basis of Karma i.e. the castes which do the unclean work like leather work or washing of dirty clothes, or cleaning the latrines are ranked in a lower position than those others which do not perform such tasks. Washing of dirty clothes particularly the bloodstained clothes of menses and other poluted clothes of rites-de-passages, is regarded as the most unclean type of work and what is why the Dhobis are regarded as the lowest caste.

But according to another more popular theory i.e. the theory of food habit the Chamars, the Doms and the Mehtars who take beef and carion are regarded even lower to the Dhobis. Thus, each of the scheduled castes of this area to establish its superiority over others by various arguments advantageous to one, but on the actual observation it has been seen that there is no interdinning among one and another nor there is acceptance of food and drink from one side (excepting the Pasi at whose hand all other members of the scheduled castes accept drink and also food (Chakhana) of the Todi shop on the philosophy that intoxicants recognize no caste). In this context I am in full agreement with Buchanan and hence quoting him in the following paragraph:

"......................that the washermen are not absolutely vile and are rather higher than the two last mentioned tribes. In Bengal their profession is considered as quite abominable. They are therefore one of the tribes hanging on the boundaries of vileness, but everywhere here they Brahmans who perform their ceremonies and in the western parts these Brahmans are not quite so much degraded as many Varnas but are called Chausakhis as they perform in common for four eastes the Teli, Sungris, Borasiya and Dhobis, the three first of which are rich and among impure tribes are considered as pretty high. The washermen in general are instructed by the Dasnami Sannyasis, but towards the east a few are followers of the Vaishnavas. Even there, where washermen are considered Vile (Aniya) these are allowed to be only low (Nich). Another clan has separated itself from those who wash, and these people call themselves Raj Dhobi or Saphkar. They consider themselves higher than the washers and live by making mats and cultivating the ground. It is said that in the whole district there may be 2000 families that adhere almost entirely to their profession, in which from the appearance of the people they must have little industry".

Whatever be the textual position of the Dhobis, the field observation has been that their Jajmans are very fond of them. Although they are untouchable, they have entry into the courtyard of the Brahman and on the rituals of life cycle the presence of Dhobi is taken as suspicious. People have comparatively some kind words and soft treatment for them. This may be in recognition of their useful services rendered for the masters.

The People

It has been mentioned earlier that they are scattered far and wide and seldom one finds a village where they are thickly populated. The following table will show the population pattern of Dhobi

Table No. 1

SI. No.	Head of the family	Name of village	Population
1.	Akalu safi	Kurson	9
2.	Sukan Safi	"	10
3.	Dhorai Safi	"	1
4.	Buchan Safi	"	2
5.	Kari Safi	"	9
6.	Ram Prasad Safi	"	3
7.	Jhotan Safi	Dadapatti	3
8.	Jhakai Safi	Pohaddi	4
9.	Kulkul Safi	"	6
10.	Butan Safi	Dhemuar	4
11.	Jhatilal Safi	"	6
			57

1. An Account of the district of Purnea in 1809-10 F, Buchanan, pp. 245, Govt. printing, Bihar and Orissa, Patna-1928.

Thus, it is evident from the perusal of Table No. 1 that whereas in the village of Kurson there are 6 families of Dhobi in the villages of Dadpatti, Pohaddi and Dhamuar they are 1 and 2 each in the last two villages. The average size of family is also roughly about 5 members.

Table No. 2

Table showing the distribution of population in Sex and age in years

Sl. No.	Head of family	Total	M	F	Age in years				
					0.5	6-10	11-20	21-45	46+
1.	Akalu Safi	9	5	4	1	1	2	4	1
2.	Sukan Safi	10	5	5	3	2	0	3	2
3.	Dohrai Safi	1	1	0	0	0	0	0	1
4.	Buchan Safi	2	1	1	0	0	0	2	0
5.	Kari Safi	9	5	4	2	1	1	5	0
6.	Ram Pd. Safi	3	1	2	0	1	1	1	0
7.	Jhotan Safi	3	1	2	1	0	0	2	0
8.	Jhakai Safi	4	2	2	0	0	2	2	0
9.	Kulkul Das Safi	6	3	3	0	2	0	2	2
10.	Butan Safi	4	2	2	0	0	2	2	0
11.	Jhatilal Safi	6	3	3	0	2	3	1	0
		57	29	28	7	0	11	24	6

A look into Table No. 2 reveals that in the matter of sex ratio there are 28 females for 29 males but in the age group distribution there are certain imbalances in the age groups of 0.5 years and 46 and above as the two groups are being represented by 7 and 6 persons respectively.

Economic life

The Dhobis are by and large engaged in their traditional occupation of washermen. They are landless labour and entire labour force is kept busy after washing. Although a few families have been given some land by the ex-landlords of Kurson in lieu of their services. In such case, the Dhobis are not paid anything for the routine washing of dirty clothes. However, on the eve of marriage or the birth they get free meal (Sidha) and some paddy also. In addition they get nominal rice as Khutabanh when they carry some dirty clothes for washing. They are

2. Cultural Anthropology. F.M. Keessing: New York, 1962.

3. The Politics of the Developing areas: G.A.Almond and J.S.Coleman (eds). (Princeton: Princeton University Press, 1960.

allowed to collect the dried leaves from the mango orchard and may collect Ush (indigenous Soda) from the fallowland of their Jajmans free of cost on the eve of feasts they are not only fed but the charcoal which has been produced by way of burning the fire wood is also made available to them to use it as fuel to heat the pressing iron. It goes without saying that during the harvest of paddy they are allowed Anti (bundle of paddy) in the field. Thus, the gross income from the families of ex-landlords are many. Now a days owing to urbanisation when some modern customers ask them for better washing and pressing they ask for some tips which are granted. Thus, while for ordinary wash which is locally termed as Chhantab no extra payment is required, for adding blue and pressing (Sajab) additional tips besides a few Kathas of land are expected.

Division of Labour

Although a highly developed form of division of labour is a lacking however it is present in the form of age and sex groups.

It is prime concern of washer women to collect sufficient Patlo (dried leaves) to heat the Bhatthi (local oven indigenously made for steaming the wet clothes) and also to collect sufficient stock for the rainy season.Young chidren are also of help in this venture.The wash in proper is mostly done by the male folk, the work of drying the wet clothes are done generally by the ladies with the help of children. Application of blue (indigo) and pressing iron are mostly done by the most efficient man of the family. Again delivery of cleaned clothes and collection of the dirty ones are mostly done by the female folk. To lookafter the asses, which are of immense help of the Dhobis for fetching the Ush or carrying heavy load of wet clothes from the Ghat (cleaning platform) to the place of drying are mostly the primary duty of the children.

Thus to sum up the economic life of the Dhobis it could be safely mentioned that the entire family members of the Dhobis family struggle from dawn to dusk to fill their empty belly. As by and large they are landless, they count more on their traditional occupation of washing than any other thing. Mostly they are simple, hard working, honest and sincere and seldom a Dhobi quarrels with his Jajman.

Political Organisation

Every society if it has to persist grow and develop had to formulate and develop certain mechanism for ordering the the pattern of interaction between its members, both in the microcosm. Political organisation of a people in its broadest sense consists of forces of social conformity, the institutionalised customs by which law and order maintained. 1. To Keessing "characteristic features of political organisation are a common membership and loyality, shared traditions and symbols, an internal government for group control and welfare and system of external relations". 2. Although there are innumerable other definitions of political system but I am very much tempted to quote Almond "The political system is that system of interaction to be found in all independent societies which perform the functions of integration and adaptation (both internally and eeis-a-vis other societies) by means of employment, or threat of employment, of more or less legitimate physical compulsion. "The political system is the legitimate, order maintaining or transforming system". 3. Coming to the political organisation of the Dhobis of Darbhanga district we find two political institutions; (1) traditional Dhobi caste Panchayat headed by the Manjan exclusively held by the Dhobis and (2) State sponsored Gram Panchayat run by the Mukhya and Sur Pancha. Thus, whereas the former has been a traditional institation and has helped a lot in maintaining the law and order and upkeeping the rradition at a high esteem the later is of comparatively recent origin under an Act of the State Government after India's Independence-hence the Dhobis also share this Panchayat along with all other members of the different castes present in the village. It is for this reason that the Dhobis try their best to find out the solution of their problems inside their caste panchayat which they treat as mainten or, preserver and custodian of their cultural heritage and this is why they are so fond of this panchayat.

Hence, I must confess here at the outset that the main theme of this paper has been to highlight the organisation and functions of this caste panchayat. Although there will be reference of gram panchayat too by way of comparison.

The Dhobi Ceste Panchayat

Composition: The Dhobi Jati panchayat of Kurson area is locally called as the Atha gama Dhobi Jati Sabha. Since the following eight villages-Lagma, Sakatpur, Raima, Behat, Kurson, Dhamuar,Alinagar and Pohaddi are its constituent members it is called Atha gama (of Eight villages). This is a local style common among the Harijan to address their caste panchayat by the number of the villages which are its constituent members. Thus a panchayat having 12, 16, 20 and 22 members are referred to as Barha Sorha, Beesa and Baisi panchayat respectively. It was mentioned earlier that since no where in a particular village there is sufficient Dhobi population to form a panchayat they combing a few villages of that locality having sizable population. Another point which was mentioned during the field work is that the decision arrived at by a body having more followers are taken as more proper and carries more weight and vice versa. Thus, if there were some decisions against someone and one does not like to concead to that he be compelled to obey otherwise he is threatened to a social boycott or excommunication. Thus, at times a culprit concedes in pressure and coercion which requires considerable collection of people even in the form of a group to give a vent to collective threat. This is more relevant in case of intercaste disputes particularly with the dominant castes.

A third point which has mentioned by none but I gathered by way of enquiry is that most of the Dhobi marriages take place within the range of panchayat.This has double advantages firstly the panchayat relation helps in settling the marriage and secondly the panchayat takes care about the conjugal relation too. This becomes vivid when some cases of divorce are brought before the panchayat. Since both the parties are the members of a common panchayat the panchayat takes such decisions which are best for both the parties and it is easy to execute it for the obvious reason.

Thus, to sum up the composition of the Dhobi caste panchayat this could be said that whereas there is a village caste panchayat for every Dhobi village and all the Dhobi residents are its members. This is about the composition and jurisdiction of the mini panchayat but for the maxi panchayat which has been referred to as the Atha Gama Dhobi Jatiye-Panchayat of the area under study its jurisdiction extends to the eight villages already mentioned and all the Dhobi residents of these eight villages are its members. Shri Mahabir Safi of Lagma is the head of the panchayat who is locally mentioned as the Mainjan, a corrupt of Manyajan (respected person). The post of the Mainjan is hereditory and passes from father to son. He is the solitary official having permanent position as the Chairman of the panchayat. Other members of the executive are nominated by him. Thus, he holds the supreme position in the political organisation of the Dhobis.

Jurisdiction and Function

It has been mentioned earlier also that at least one caste panchayat exists for each caste in the village, and its jurisdiction extends to all members of that caste residing in the village, its primary function is to uphold the pattern of social behaviour and the religious values of the members of that caste. It is also used to further the group interests of the caste. Here, in the case of the Dhobis, the general laws hold good with a little change that the caste panchayat of a particular village is not so powerful whereas the Atha gama Dhobi-Jatiya Panchayat is the supreme in matters important for caste. Thus, owing to thinness of its population the regional caste panchayat comprising of eight villages having Dhobi residents deals with offences connected with marriage and morals, food and drink, exchange of Hukka-pani (indigenous smoking impliment) with members of other castes and prohibited pursuits of the cases arising out of breaches of the marriage and sex regulations like seduction of wife, adultery, immorality, concubinage, breach of promise of marriage, refusal to perform Gauna ceremony and divorce. Sometime a newly married young wife takes to heel from her husband's house and its recurrence is taken as a serious matter and an old matter of love affair is very often diagnosed as a causes of the fled and hence this is also well within the jurisdiction of the panchayat. Infringment of the caste customs in matters of the disposal of the dead or feast to castemen is also dealt with. If there has been any irregularity in the Jajmani relationship like abrupt change of the Kamin or Jajman without the proper process or stoping the rights and privileges to the Kamins by the Jajmans, this is also within the purview of the caste panchayat. Jajmani rights can not be transferred without the approval of the caste panchayat. Similarly, if one is found guilty for violating some sacred or social norms like killing cow, cat etc. or has insulted the Brahmin one is punished by the panchayat. If there has been a theft in the house of a Dhobi or there has been an accident of fire in the Bhatthi in which a large number of clothes are burnt and the customers are not satisfied with the explanation of the Dhobi, the matter may be referred to the caste panchayat. But in this meeting some important customers of the Brahmin caste also participate and the meeting will generally be held at the Khalihan (thrashing ground) of some ex-landlord of Kurson.

Again in the matter of witchcraft and contagious diseases like small pox or cholera an urgent meeting of the panchayat is summoned to check the outbreak at earliest. The Dhobis are very often the early prey of the epidemics because they have to wash the dirty clothes and some of which may have the insects of infectious diseases and also of the epidemics.

The division of the joint family leading quarrels also comes well within the jurisdiction of the caste panchayat. These are mostly settled by the village caste panchayat. Seldom a separation case is brought and tried by the Atha gama panchayat.

Sometimes some minor cases of eveteasing by teenager are also brought in the panchayat. One Ram Prasad Safi a resident of Kurson was found guilty of teasing girls while they were taking bath in a village tank. The matter was firstly brought before the elderly persons who gave a warning to Ram Prasad. But as he did not refrain from doing the same the local Dhobi panchayat of Kurson summoned a meeting in which Ram Prasad was found guilty of teasing the girls and was ordered to arrange a feast of all the members of all the Dhobi villages by way of fine failing which the matter would be referred to the Atha gama panchayat with a recommendation in general not to marry the younger sister of the culprit. No sooner it was decided in the panchayat Ram Prasad arranged a caste feast before the matter took a serious turn.

Trail and Punishment

It should be mentioned at the very outset that as by and large the Dhobis are illiterate they do not believe in recording the statments either of Muddai (aggrieved) or a Mudalah (defendent). There is no written law but old precidence are very often cited. Both the parties are made to speak at the face of each other and when one has finished the Manijan would like to know from the opposition party whether whatsoever one is saying is correct or not and what the defendent has to say in the defence. Thus, by doing so and chiding every one even the witnesses tell only the truth in which stick may also be used to confess the guilt, the panchas arrive at a general consensus about the actual culprit and the nature and the nature and magnitude of offence done against the aggrieved.

Fine to be realised in cash and to be spent over the maintenance of repair of some community institution like the temple of Durga or Salhesh or to be given the aggrieved as compensation or to be spent over the community feast is the most common punishment. Sometimes if the offence is much which demands the corporal punishment to terrorise others as a preventive measure and pleases the sentiment of the aggrieved, canning in public was also allowed in the past. Some times if the fine is heavy and the culprit is not in a position to pay them in that case he might be given option of public canning. But now with the growth of self respect this short of punishment is seldom undergone.

Observation

With the inception of a state hospital at Kurson, establishment of state sponsored gram panchayat at Kurson, opening of a few police station at Manigachhi and improvement of road communication from a Kachcha road to metalled road and regular bus survices on the road from Darbhanga to thanshyampur people have become more law abiding and have come under the purview of the formal law of the country rather than the customary practices of folk. Thus, owing to the factors mentioned above the crude method of severe punishment has lost ground by now. If any person is not satisfied with the judgement of the panchayat one is free to go to the gram panchayat whose door is always wide open to entertain all such cases. Thus, gradually the Dhobi caste panchayat which was once so powerful has been reduced to almost functionally non-existent. Now a days its decisions are binding only for those who are too poor to go even to gram panchayat. The gram panchayat admits new cases of caste importance either at initial stage or at the stage of appeal. It is commonly held even by the Dhobis that the gram panchayat has more of formal powers and its decisions are binding without any caste limitation hence currently the Dhobis have also shown their preference for the gram panchayat to their traditional Atha gama Dhobi Jati panchayat. Thus, it is for them to decide whether they prefer to abadon their traditional caste panchayat which is fast decaying or there is a collective effort to revive it.

CHANGING STATUS OF A WIDOW FROM VEDIC TO MODERN PERIOD

S.A.T. ADILAKSHMI

ABSTRACT

This paper mainly deals with the changing position of a widow from different periods that were flooded in the land of Hindu Indian Society. The necessity of the position of the widow in Hindu society particularly to a research worker in social sciences can hardly be exaggerated. Even if a Society adopts a contumelious attitude toward its women, the mother, daughter, wife are loved because of eertain important natural instincts. Generally in partriarchal dominated societies in India the Mother, Wife and Daughter are honoured it is because of the affection, status and position, of widow is entirely varied. Even though the parents are living, widows have to depend upon their husbands families.

In Vedic age "Widowhood" was not a good creature and an object of pity. So also in the epic period, a widows sorrow is equated to the sorrow of a person who has lost his male child. Hence, we may conclude that a widows sorrow was not considered to be the greatest grief by the concerned group of society. In fact her grief was the conseqeence of the past deeds in her previous incarnations. According to the Puranas and the Smrities she is not excluded from various type of Vratas as an inauspicious animal. For instance, Kunti Devi, wife of Panduraja, king of the pandaya Dynasty accompanies Droupadi to witness her marriage with her five sons, the Pandava Princes. In the similar manner Sita Devi is decked by her Mother-in-law prior to the innovation ceremony of

Sri Rama, the great epic hero of the Ramayana. By observing all these instances, we can find that they were not considered the widow as inauspicious and excluded from auspicious and religious ceremonies.

– S.A.T. ADILAKSHMI, Research Scholar, Deptt. of Sociology
S.V. University, TIRUPATI.

4

RAJA SALHESH THE SUPREME GOD OF THE DUSADH : BARARI A CASE STUDY

The village of Barari falls within the block Barari under the district of Katihar in Bihar. So far the boundary of the village is concerned the Ganga Darjeeling road passes on the Eastern side whereas on the West flows the river Barandi - a tributary of Koshi. The National High Way No. 31 passes on the Northern side of the village and Karhagola Railway station lies on the Southern side of the village. Barari Block is situated at a distance of 2 Km. south of the village.

The village of Barari has several tolas but the Dusadhs live two tolas namely, Bharati tola and Laxmipur Dusadh toli. In each toli there are twenty houses of Dusadhs containing twenty families. Thus, in total the village of Barari is inhabited by 40 families of Dusadh excluding other Harijan and Upper caste people.The total population of the Dusadh is 295 only out of which the number of male is 175 and that of female it is 120 only.The distribution of Dusadh population into various age and sex groups is given below in a tabular form :

Table No. 1

Age group	*Male*	*Female*	*Total*	*Percentage*
1	*2*	*3*	*4*	*5*
1-5	26	21	47	16.18
6-10	20	18	38	13.21
11-15	23	13	36	11.99
16-20	16	10	25	8.46
21-30	40	23	63	21.01
31-40	22	19	41	14.20
41-50	17	9	26	8.60
51-Above	12	7	19	6.35
Total	175	120	295	100.00

Thus, it is vivid from the perusal of Table No. 1 that the number of male exceed that of female in all the age groups.This adverse sex ratio among the Dusada of Barari may reveal many interesting demographic facts which are beyond the scope of this paper.

Who are the Dusadhs ?

Tracing the origin of the Dusadh one has to go back to the origin of caste itself according to which the Dusadhs are of the Shudra origin which has later on called as Harijan-Constitutionally the Dusadhs are one of 23 communities declared as the Scheduled Castes in the State of Bihar. The Dusadhs are not happy about their low caste status nor they are satisfied with the award of Harijan offered to them by Bapu. They claim that they are of the Kshatriya origin which they support by the following legends:

According to a legend current among some sections of the Dusadhs they are the descendants of the great Kaurava king Dussashan. The Kauravas were responsible for the dreadful war of Mahabharat, and their descendants were cursed to become an object of hate and destitute. The Kauravas were of lunar origin (Chandra Bansi) and the Dusadhs also claim to be of Chandra Bansi Kshatriya origin.

Another legend puts the Dusadhs under the caste of the Gahlot Rajputas.This is a very widely known myth which says that during the time of king Shiladitya one Ballimipur the capital city of the then Rajasthan, was attacked by enemy. The king Shiladitya was killed in this war. And as per convention, except queen Puspavati who was then in the family way his several wives burnt themselves alive in order to perform Jauhar or Sati. Puspavati escaped to the Maliya range and got shelter there. After sometime a son was born to her. As the boy was born in Guha (Cave) he was named as Goha which means born in a cav. Later on Goha was called by the names of Gohaditya, Guhil and Guhadhtta. Goha was brought up by Kamlavati (a Brahmin woman) as Puspavati the mother of Goha, died. Goha was a very sharp minded boy who managed to get the estate of Idur from the King Mandalik who was by then very old. Mandalik, a Bhil by tribe, was later on killed by Goha. Goha had now a clean sailing. His descendents adopted this name for the gotra of all the members of that bansha (root).This practice continued till the year 1257 A.D. when Rahup a Gahlout managed to regain his ancestoral kingdom of Chittor from the king of Kalour.There were two main changes during his regime. The first was the adoption of Sisodiya gotra as a substitute for the Gahilot and the second was the change in the title from Rahup to Rana. Again roughly after two hundred years in the year 1439 when Rana Lakha was drowned there were sporadic risings of the Mughal in various places of the Eastern India. It is interesting to note that the sacred city of Gaya was also attacked by the Mughals and Rana Lakha (Lax Singh) had brought an army of selected brave Rajputas to purge out the enemy from the sacred soil of Gaya. Rana Lakha was killed in the battle field at Gaya while chasing the enemy. It is believed that the town of Lakhisarai (old name Lakhi Dera) in the district of Monghyr was then founded to commemorate the Yomans service of Lakha Singh. After the death of Lakha Singh there was some confusion in his army organisation. A section of his army preferred to stay in Bihar to protect the Hindu sacred shrines against Muslim invasion whereas others were forced to stay in this very geographical area as their retreat to Rajasthan was not possible due to communicational problems. Hence, this race of Sisodiya Rajput settled in and around Gaya, and in course of time they migrated to other parts of Bihar. The original Gahlot branched off into the following 24 branches: 1. Ahriya, 2. Mangolia, 3. Sisodiya, 4. Pipra, 5. Kailaya, 6. Guhner, 7. Chorniaya, 8. Godab, 9. Majropa, 10. Bhimla, 11. Kankot, 12. Kotecha, 13. Sora, 14. Uhar, 15. Useba, 16. Nirup, 17. Nadodya, 18. Nadhota, 19. Bhojkara, 20. Kuchera, 21. Dusadh, 22. Bhetbara, 23. Paha and 24. Purot of these many branches of the Gahlots are no longer found anywhere.

Dusadhs and their Divisions

Dusadhs are sub-divided into the following eleven sub-branches: 1. Maghaiya, 2. Kamur, 3. Paliwar, 4. Baburch, 5. Kurin, 6. Silontha, 7. Surjha, 8. Kanoujia, 9. Bahalia, 10. Madeshiya and 11. Dharhi.

Social history of the Dusadh

The Dusadhs have eleven sub-castes and two common titles Paswan and Das Paswan is the most common title whereas Das has certain status value. Das is normally affixed with the names of such persons who are either Kabir Panthi or Ojha Gunees, or otherwise elevated from the commonars. In the urban areas sometimes they have been found using such titles as Prasad and Singh. Dusadh informant very proudly explained me that the very meaning of the term Dusadh is the one difficult to be controlled and the Paswan title also refers to heroic deeds the protector or a strong watchman.

The social history of the Dusadh is the history of opression exploitation, met with over the centuries. It is said that during the Mughal rule the Dusadhs were tortured and their young women were raped and kidnapped by the Muslims. To protect the chastity of their woman they adopted two protective measures firstly, they gave their daughters in marriage at an early age, even before five years and secondly, they started rearing pigs on large scale so they could chase the Muslims with the help of pigs at the various sight of the pigs the Muslims would run away. Further more, protective measure, the Dusadhs began eating pork, and their unmarried girl is required to put on a small piece of the bone of a pig in the form of a tabij round has neck. The Dusadh informants held that they are the descendants of the Gahlot Rajputs, and hence their girls are more fair in complexion than those of any other Harijan community, but this beauty was a curse for them during the Moughal period. To make their beautiful girls ugly, so as to save them from the cruel. hands of the rapacious Muslims, they started tatooing (Godna) on most of the exposed parts of their body.

Economically the Dusadhs are very backward. They are landless in true sense and to earn their wage as the casual agricultural labour is their main source of livelihood. Educationally and politically also they are equally backward. They are very orthodox people and believe in the working of fats to a very great extent. They are very superstitions and believe in the existence of spirit ghost, witchcraft and several deities and demi-gods.

Raja Salhesh

The Dusadhs of Barari have a separate set of divinity headed by Rajaji or Salhesh Maharaj along with all the gods and deities worshipped by the members of upper castes. They regard Salhesh as their supreme deity. In Barari there is a small Gahbar (temple) of Salhesh made of thatched roof in a corner of the village. There are four terracotta images of males and one of female in the temple. Rajaji is scated on an elephant, three other images are those of chuharnial a famous wrestler and the military secretary of Salhesh, the third image is that of Moti Ram who is said to be his brother, and the fourth image is of Karikant who is his nephew (sister's son) and these two fallows are his body guards.The solitary female image is of Dauna Malin who loved Rajaji.

Legend Regarding the Origin of Salhesh Maharaj

There are various folktales and stories told by the Dusadhs about the origin of Rajaji the most popular legend is given below:

Once some ashes from the Yajna of Brahma fall from heaven to river Ganges. No sooner the ashes fall they were converted into a beautiful lotus flower. Some girls from Raja Pakaria family want for a bath in the river and they were attracted to see that flower. All the girls tried their best to pluck the a beautiful flower but in vain. Tired of her efforts, one of the girls lastly spread her Anchal of Sari as a symbol of adoration and prayer and then the lotus came into her fold. Then she plucked the flower and came home happily. She kept the flower on her bed and came out to wash her feet before going to bed. When she returned back to her bed to her surprise she found a handsome boy playing on the bed instead of the lotus flower. She was very much afraid of this. When she narrated the event to her parents they refused to believe her and thought that the daughter was sinner hence she must be killed.The parents arranged some fire wood to burn her alive. When the pyre was ready she was made to sit over it with the boy in her lap it was set on fire.The wood burnt without any sign of burning to them. In the process of burning there was one more miracle the newly born baby was changed into a boy six months old and was seen sucking milk from the breast of the girl to the surprise of the parents of the girl they saw the boy changing the forms of parrot, tiger and the like. Thus, they thought

1. The Castes and Tribes of N.W. Provinces and Oudh. Crooke, W, Vol. IV: 138-152, Calcutta, 1896.

that they might be killed by the powerful magic boy as such all of them fled away from that place. The boy grew up into a very strong man in due course of time and he was later on named as Sallesh Maharaj or Rajaji as the Dusadhs call him. Another popular belief common among the Dusadhs is that Raja Salhesh had his ancestoral home in Phulbari near Biratnagar of Nepal where there is a very old temple of Salhesh which is a place of pilgrimage for the Dusadhs of Bihar and also of those who live in the Tarai area of Nepal.

Raja Salhesh is believed to be all powerful, omnipresent omnipotent and there is nothing beyond his capacity should be like to do anything there is no power on this earth which can prevent him in doing so. The Dusadhs tell various stories of his greatness, goodness and generosity. Salhesh is a vegetarian deity hence no animal is sacrificed. He likes laddu and pan. Milk pudding is his favourite food.

It has been mentioned earlier that economically they are very poor people hence they cannot be lavish in worshipping Salhesh but from their adoration and other hearty offerings it is vivid that the Dusadhs of Barari are very fond of their supreme lord Rajaji whom they cannot forget even for a moment. Once in a year the Dusadhs celebrate Salhesh puja at the village level, generally in the month of Baisakh or Shravan, when they collect subscriptions from all the Dusadh families. The members of other upper castes also offer subscription generously, Salhesh is worshipped ceremonially with great excitement and pomp.

Conclusion

The Dusadhs of Barari regard Salhesh as their supreme God. He is believed to be possessed with divine strength and is capable of granting good health and sufficient strength to his devotees. The Dusadhs being a band of landless agricultural labourer count upon their strength and health alone by virtue of which they can earn their bread and hence the Dusadh's veneration to Salhesh as their supreme deity is but natural.

5

FAMILY AND MARRIAGE AMONG THE PASIS OF DARBHANGA

The Pasis are one of the 23 Scheduled Castes of the State of Bihar having a total population of 46360 out of which 239762 are males and rest of 223839 females as per census of 1971. Numerically this is the 5th major Scheduled Caste but traditionally this is the only community dealing in Today trapping and has monopoly in its trade.

Origin of the Pasis

Traditionally the Pasis are of the Sudra Varna, a caste of untouchable like the Dusadh, the Musahar and the Khatwe but it appears that since they deal in liquor, in their case, their untouchability is not so strictly observed as those of others. Now there are many a popular stories told by them regarding their origin and affiliation to several goddess and saints like Bhagabati and Balmiki respectively. A few stories are given below:

(i) The Pasis of Darbhanga having a population of 13,703 persons claim that they are the descendents of Maharashi Valmiki Ratnakar, Ratnakar was a highway robber who would loot and murder the passers by after he had snatched everything. He sold neera (unfermented juice of date and palm) to keep himself engaged. Once he happened to see a saint who advised him to recite the name of Lord Rama but as a murderer he was not convinced, thus the saint advised him to recite mara mara chainlessly. This was acceptable to Ratnakar and he started reciting this very sincerely. It is believed that Ratnakar was lost in trance in the process of recitation and thus the white ant surrounded him. Lord Rama, gave him a Darshan, being pleased by his penance after which he was called Valmiki (a mountain of white ant). Valmiki later on wrote the immortal Ramayana. Thus, these Pasis claim their ancestory in the great epic author, Valmiki.

(ii) Another interesting story of the origin of the Pasi is that lived a carpenter in a certain village. He used to tell people that he lived a carpenter in a certain village. He used to tell people that he was immortal as he had designed a cage to capture the Yama. When the Yama came to entrap the carpenter in his hook he went inside the cage. Yama followed him. The carpenter was so cunning that he escaped the cage through a secret exit instead arrested the Yama in his cage and locked him.There was great panic and confusion in the heaven when all the Gods failed to trace the Yama they approached goddess Bhagwati collectively to search for the Yama. Bhagwati had to accept the challenge. She adopted a novel method of spying. She opened a Toddy shop on this earth.Very soon this shop became very popular. One day the carpenter also came to drink there. After drinking the Toddy he became tipsy and divulged the secret of captivating the Yama. She was posing as if she was not convinced on this the drunken carpenter invited her to follow him where he showed her not only the cage but the method of opening its door too. No sooner they left the place, Bhagwati who was in disguise of a Pasin went back again and set the Yama free by opening its door and instantly the carpenter died. Since goddess Bhagwati was first to sell the Toddy the Pasis claim to be her offspring.

Besides these two empirical stories regarding their origin I would like to mention two more popular versions regarding the derivation of the name Pasi as recorded by Crooke. According to one of the versions etemologically the term 'Pasi' is derived from the Sanskrit Pashika, meaning one who uses a noose, as used by Pasi for climbing the palm tree for toddy tapping. According to another version, which was found more popular among the Pasi, their name has "One day a men was going to kill a number of cows. Parsurama was at that time practising austerities in the jungles. Hearing the cries of the sacred animals he rushed to their assistance. But the cow killer was aided by his friends. So Parsurama made five men out of Kusa grass and brought them to life by letting drops of his perspiration fall upon them. Hence, arose the name Pasi from the "Hindi pasina 'sweat' (Sanskrit Prasrinna", covered with perspiration").The men thus created rescued the Cows.[2]

2. Ibid

Again, the Kaith was a sub-caste of the Pasi has an extension of the legend about their origin. As has been seen that five men were created by Parsuram to rescue the cows. They returned after rescuing the cows and asked Parsurama for a wife. Just at that moment a Kayastha girl was passing by and Parsurama seized her and handed over to the five Pasis. Their offsprings came to be regarded as Kaithwas Pasi.

There is yet another section of Pasi namely the Rajpasi and legend about their origin as recorded by crooke is given below :

"....The ancestor of the tribe was one is Rattan Daksha. When Parsuram destroyed the Kshtriyas, he killed Raja Vena as well as others and then the Rani kept the corpse of her husband and implored Parsurama create a man to continue the race, Parsurama touched the head of Raja Vena and out of it sprang a man of dark complexion with a bow and arrow in his hand. He was the first Rajpasi and he was entrusted the duty of watchman and Kingdom."[3]

Thus, it is vivid from the perusal of several empirical folk tables and also myths collected by Crooke that the Pasis like other Harijan communities try to establish this ancestory with kings and saints. The fact that now the Pasis lay emphasis to prove their Kshatrya ancestar shows that they make use of mythology for justifying their supposed glorious kshatriya origin which serves them as a too in their social upward movement.

Sub-Castes

There are various sub-castes of Pasi found all over India. Some of them appear to be common in several provinces, but most of these are regional in distribution, for example, Tirsuli one of the sub-castes are found in Binar, U.P. and M.P. but Rajpasi, Gujar, Baurasi, Bhar Kaithmas and like are found in U.P. and M.P. but not in Bihar, Risley had spotted as many nine following subcastes in the Bihar:- (i). Kamani, (ii). Gaiduha, (iii). Byadha, (iv). Tirsuliya, (v). Mangta, (vi). Chiriyamar, (vii). Chudchadha, (viii). Baheliya and Khatik.

3. Ibid.

During my field work among the pasis of Darbhanga in north Bihar however, I could find out only four following sub-castes of Pasi :

(i) Tarsulia or Tirsulia- this was a sub-caste by skinning off the upper surface of the trunk of date and palm trees. Thus, this is the only section of entire pasi population which is engaged in their age old traditional occupation. The people of this group take goddess Bhagawati as their protector, hence in almost every act either ascending up a date tree or descending from the same and also while drinking the toddy they spell out of following brief prayer "As you have extricated Yama Raja by the discovery of toddy, so keep me always out of danger and difficulties".

(ii) Kamari- The literal meaning of Kamani is a bow which has its association with hunting. Thus, this sub-caste of pasi chose hunting as

4. Tribes and Castes of Bengal: Risley H.H. Vol.II:166-168 Calcutta-1861.

Their traditional occupation, or those who showed proficiency in hunting gradually became a sub-caste having traditional occupation of hunting.

(iii) Gaiduha- This is again a sub-caste which specialised in milching the cows. It appears that some of them took the profession of domestication of cows and their milching and in due course of time they were declared as Gaiduha-pasi.

(iv) Byadha- As per meaning of the term those who retained the profession of traping birds and hunting other games were called the Byadha from among the Pasi.

From the perusal of the foregoing few paragraphs it appears that the various sub-castes of the Pasis are very much evolved and they strictly adhere to their investigation reveals that now there is only one occupation of toddy tapping followed by all the sub-castes. All the four sub-castes are endogamous groups and it is only at the time of matrimonial relation they remember their sub-caste otherwise they prefer to be called as Balmiki. There has been a tendency to conceal one's caste name among the Harijan. For example, the Chamar, the Dom, the Musahar and the Pasi would like to be addressed as Ravidas, Choudhary, Rikhiashan and Balmiki respectively then their caste names affixed at the end of their surnames which has been prevalent till recently. I take it as a pointer of dynamism which might help them in their assimilation into the Hindu fold of society.

Ethnographic details

The present study is based on the field work among the Pasi of north Bihar. The author surveyed the Pasis of the districts of Patna, Gaya, Bhagalpur and Muzaffurpur in general and Darbhanga in particular. For such accounts as rites de passage, social and political aspects data collected from the survey have been utilised for the demographic details it is based on a sample of 50 families of 390 persons of five villages Lakshmisagar Gangwara, Sara Mohanpur, Kabir chak and Kila ghat around the district town of Darbhanga. The Pasis are so sporadically distributed that a researcher has to cover quite a big area to have a workable sample for the demographic treatment. The distribution of the Pasi population can be seen from the perusal of the Table No. 1 given below:

Table No. 1

Name of the Villages	Total Population	Male	Female
1. Lakshmisagar	117	65	52
2. Kabir chak	92	43	49
3. Kilaghat	65	35	30
4. Gangwara	72	37	35
5. Saramohanpur	24	16	8
	370	196	174

Thus, it is clear from the perusal of Table No. 1 mentioned above that the males out number the female. It is only in the village of Kabirchak that the females out number the males. But coming to Saramohanpur one finds the sex ratio miserably adverse as there are only 8 females for 16 males.

Family and Marriage

Family and marriage are essential institutions universally distributed in all over the world and the Pasis are not exception to this. They live in the patriarchal family. In composition most of the families are nuclear as 39 families out of 50 were the nuclear families whereas joint and extended families were represented only by 11 families. Thus, 73 percent of the families under sample were the nuclear and rest of 22 percent joint and extended.

A pasi family is a basic and primary production consumption unit and all the members share a common roof and hearth in a kitchen. Perhaps the most important thing from their point of view has been mentioned earlier that they live in a patriarchal family apparantly the eldest male member becomes the leader of the family. He has to think and decide about all the affairs of his family and other have to follow him.

The Pasis live in a separate toli popularly known as Pasi toli. No other person of clean castes, very often, even the Harijan does not like to live by Pasi toli which they regard as area of quarrel and corruption. It is believed that a drunken man behaves abnormally hence a person who loves prestige and peace should build his house as far as possible from the Pasi toli. The Pasis are conditioned to all these and they also want some secrecy even for this business. A regular visitor of the Pasi Toli is taken to be a man of doubtful character. Generally, the pasi's live in a thatched house with and wall. Most of the houses are such which have two rooms and two varandah one of which is inner and another as outer. The rooms are used for the purpose of sleeping and also storing the articles of daily use. The inner varandah, which is a arrow as compared to the cutter, is used for kitchen and dinning and also for sleeping of the women folk during the hot summer nights. The outer varandah is both a Dalan for sitting and sleeping purposes and it houses the Tari-Khanaita. One can find several vats of fermented toddy and many small Lavani (a small earthen pot to measure toddy) and a few dirty and multicoloured tubblers for drinking toddy and some Chakhnairag (snack) surrounded with the innumerable flies in a Tari-khana. It is a peculiar place having no parallel nor even resemblences with any other institution. The customers are very often fixed persons. It is only a Barat party and rarely a stranger that a Pasi khana receives new faces. The shop keeper knows the nature and economic condition of the customers and deals them accordingly.

The family life of a Pasi is the same as of any other scheduled caste with the difference that here the female folk can also sit in the pasikhana and sell the toddy. It was observed that since the male Pasi had to go round the date and palm trees to save the tender portion of the tree and to change the pots twice daily the female folk managed the shop. They were comparatively better and cleaner clothes and had certain silver ornaments on their persons. Since they had small business they cared for the food, health and in some cases education of their children. The Pasi women preferred to sit in the pasikhana and sell toddy than to go outside to work as a casual labour or agricultural labour. In the schools also a large number of Pasi children were seen. Thus, the family life of the pasi appears to be harmonious however, on certain occasion when the husband becomes a habitual drankard the wife was reported to be of cross nature and of quarrel some temperament, the family life was disturbed.

Marriage

The Pasis live in a part society because rarely one can find a village having entirely Pasi population. Normally the composition of the village is of mixed type having bulk of the population of upper castes, a few families of Backward communities and Harijans. Thus, there are several models before the pasis to follow. They regard marriage as the most important ritual event of the life of an individual which is witnessed by the festivity and celebration associated with the marriage. This is rather the happiest occasion of their life they like to share with their relations and friends.The need for marriage is attributed to biological need, procreation and economic cooperation of the husband and wife.

They have a system of sub-caste endogamy but they must marry outside the gotra and in no case a marriage can take place within the kinsmen. They have been practising child marriage. But now owing to modernity they have also shown a preference for the adult marriage but even then the average age of marriage for the girls would come to

15 years. Their preference for the adult marriage is partially due to the marriage expences. Traditionally they had a system of token bride price in kind like a few pieces of sari, some rice, sweets and some materials for the marriage feast. But a large section of them who are comparatively better off have switched over to the system of dowry. Which is in the vouge among the upper caste people. Thus, now in urban areas they have adopted the dowry system, also the rural better off people have been drifting towards dowry, but the rural uneducated and poor Pasi people still adhere to the age old system of bride price.Thus those who still maintain the system of bride price practice child marriage and other who believe in the dowry system practise adult marriage.

The Pasis are by and large monogamous people but one can have plural wives if one has resources to maintain or the first wife is barren or a witch but in either case they approved to obtain a second wife is essential. Widow remarriage is allowed. Divorce with the consent of the panchayat is possible and the remarriage of the divorced persons allowed by the approval of the panchayat. No bride price and dowry is required in the cases of re-marriages. The function is simple but it has the sanction of society.

Coming to the marriage negotiation it is interesting to note that the groom party has to initiate the talk. A group of five or seven elderly persons visits the house of the prospective bride. This visit is pre-planned as such on their arrival they are served with Hukka Pani and Bidi Supari. Thus, the leader of the team who is normally the father, elder brother, or the maternal uncle initiates the talk by explaining the purpose of their visit. Regarding the suitability of the couple they have only one consideration i.e. the height of the two.The groom should be taller than the bride. Since they keep no horoscope, the exact age either of the bride or of groom is not known nor they do care much about the matching of age because most of the marriage are settled in the childhood. They keep the measurement of the height of the groom in a stick, naturally when the party has initiated the talk, and the bride's parents like the negotiation the bride is measured with the stick. If the bride is taller the negotiation fails, if shorter or of the same stature both the parties discuss the issue and settle the negotiation. Negotiation may also fail if there is no compromise on the issue of the size of the Barat party and bride price or the dowry as the case may be. Sarbat and tea may be served in the process of negotiation. If the marriage negotiation has a favourable chance the visiting team may be fed with Churagur or the meal itself. They may be offered today at last. When all these are over the leader of the team would formally ask the father or the guardian of the bride in question whether they have liked the negotiation and they are willing to give the bride in marriage. When the bride party has consented, the leader of the team would invite them for the Ghar-Dekhee inspection of the grooms house, when this date has been fixed the visiting team goes back in a happy mood. Now it is the turn of the bride's party to visit the groom's house. After a week or so of the visit of the grooms party the bride's party with a few elderly persons repay the visit of the groom's house where they are received ceremonially and treated in the same manner as they had been at the bride's house.

Now when each party has seen other's house and both of them to be agreable on the conditions of the marriage, a date of marriage, which suits both the parties, is fixed. The Pasis regard Aghan, Magh and Phagun as auspicious months for the marriage. As such any date between Aghan to Phagun is fixed for the marriage. Thus, the bride party goes back, As has been mentioned earlier that Pasis live in part society, the impact of the Sanskritic rites and rituals of the Brahminic Hinduism are visible there. On the arrival of the Barat at bride's house the groom is taken to the village deity for Pranam (Sallutation) thus other rituals like Matkor, Aam-Mahu-Biyah etc. take place. Thus, both the groom and bride are brought to vedi where a Brahman Purohit officiates the marriage. He supervises the function and chants some Mantras and Shlokas. A few ceremonies namely, ghunghat Niriksh- man, Uttangar, Kanyadan, Nakbedi, Sindur dan are officiated by the Brahman Pandit. Most of these rituals are Brahminic. Their indigeneous ritual which is perhaps the most important and universal is ritual of Kumari-Lahchhu.The Pasis believe the relationship of the husband and wife as those of blood and to stablise this they have a custom of Lahchhu. This is the custom of licking the virgin blood, for which the little finger of the left hand of the bride is pricked and the bride groom has to lick this blood, and in turn the little finger of the left hand of the groom is pricked and this time the bride has to lick the blood. This blood licking ceremony is observed with a great enthusiasm by the Pasis with the belief that this mixing of the blood of the two bodies the two souls, are combined into one and thus they become inseparable afterwards. After the marriage ceremony is over the persons of the Barat party officially see the face of bride and offer some money. The next morning the Barat party leaves after breakfast along with the newly weded couple. As has been mentioned earlier that they practise child marriage the bride comes back to her parents house within afew days, where she stays on till she attains puberty in a few years. She goes to the house of her husband on the eve of the Dwiragman (second marriage) after which she lives in the house of her husband with his kinsmen, sharing the joys and sorrows of life with her husband's sib.

Divorce and Remarriage

Divorce, although not very common is not unknown among them. They do not encourage this system because once it is allowed even on genuine grounds other may demand this for trifling matter. However, if the wife turns up for adultary or is defamed for being a witch divorce could be possible after seeking the permission of the caste Panchayat. Similarly if a husband turns up drunkard or develop sexual intimacy with other women and does not maintain his wife properly the husband could also be divorced with the permission of the caste panchayat. As divorce so desertion is also found among them. The spouse feeling that conspiracy of the partner is not congenial, may desert the other without the consent of the panchayat the charges here are vegue and not established.

Remarriage of the divorced spouse may be possible but is difficult for obvious reason. But widow remarriage for both man and woman is very common because they do not assign any fault with individual. In case of widow remarriage also they do not encourage the aged widow. Normally a widow has to remarry a widower of a compatable age. Sometime if a widower is above want and if he so likes he can marry a virgin girl. In cases of widow remarriage the rituals are simple and limited but a few caste men may be fed.

The Pasis of Darbhanga are of Sudra origin. There are several interesting stories about their origin. They are divided into many sub-castes and at least four of them were identified during the field work. Toddy tapping is their main traditional occupation. Almost every member of the family is kept busy in the trade of toddy. Family is the basic unit of production and by and large there is good understanding and cooperation among the members of the family. The institution of marriage is very important which helps them to lead a regular and contested conjugal life. Needless to mention that their economic compulsiveness in which the husband is a collector and wife a seller imparate somewhat better division of labour and higher economic status to ladies as compared to many Harijan communities.

6

THE MUSAHARS AND THEIR DEENA - BHADRI

The State of Bihar is the home of more than eight millions of Harijans which is about 14 percent of the total population of the state. There are 23 Scheduled castes communities which taken together constitute this total population of Harijan. The Musahar is the third largest scheduled caste having a total population of 1391000 persons in Bihar. Although they are found in small number in each area of Bihar but their main concentration is in the north Bihar particularly in the districts of Purnea, Monghyr, Saharsa and Darbhanga.

The Musahars are the most primitive scheduled caste of Bihar. There are several views about their origin. Commonly people believe that they are a branch of the Bhuiya (a tribe) but Hunter is of opinion. The Musahars are generally considered to be a branch, which has out grown its parent stem of the once important Tharu people, who ruled in Northen Oudh and the country eastward to the Gandak, whence they were driven by the great Aryan movement usually known as the Rajput invasion. How they extend India is now unknown: but they are supposed, from their likeness from the eastern hill men, to have come from the north east. Dr. Buchanan Hamilton says of them. “They retain in their features strong marks of a Chinese or Tartar Origin”. People believe that the word Musahar is the combination of two terms Musa Ahar meaning there by rat-eater. The food habit of the band attests the worth of the name of the caste because the Musahars are very fond of eating rats. It is a band of landless agricultural labourers having a very good proficiency in the earth work. They are expert earth workers particularly in heavy earth work of digging tank, making road and embarkments. Thus, while digging the earth if per chance they find some rates they kill them to eat their neat.

The Musahars are always identifiable and distinguished from other Harijan communities because of its dark black skin colour, medium to short height, small opening of eye and a peculiarly typical dialect they speak. They are true to their words and love a collective life. Economically, educationally and also politically they are backward even among the Harijan. They are very orthodox and superstitious people and believe in a number of gods and goddesses some of which is of upper caste Hindus and others are of the Musahars exclusively. Each of the scheduled castes has a set of its indigenous Gods and spirits headed by one supreme God for that community, for example, if you ask a Chamar, about the supreme God one will reply veer, the Dusadh and the Musahar will name Raja Salhesh and Deena Bhadri respectively as their supreme Gods who protect them from all evils. As religion has two aspects belief in some thing, and rites dedicated to that belief. It has been mentioned that the Musahar believe that Deena Bhadri is their supreme Goa, hence popular stories as told by the Musahar about life and works of Deena Bhadri are given below: In ancient time, there lived a king named Raja Kanak Singh in the Kingdom of Jogia. He had two sisters Jadua and Bachua.

These two sisters were wicked magicians who would harm the subjects of the kingdom by magic and witchcraft.The people of the kingdom of Jogia were very sad and unhappy with the misrule of Kanak Singh. There lived an old couple of musahar Kalu Sardar and his wife Nirso Devi within the kingdom. They had two sons Deena and Bhadri. These two brothers were very brave and mighty and possessed supernatural power. They helped their castemen and others who needed them. Thus, they became darling to all the poors and downtrodden of that kingdom and the people were very proud of Deena Bhadri.This popularity of Deena Bhadri made king Kanak Singh jealous of them and her two sisters also did not like them.

Once there was a bumper crop at Jogia. When the crop was ready for the harvest Kanak Singh instructed one Badalu Chamar to announce by beating the drum in whole of Jogia Raj that harvesting was compulsory for all, in the farms of the king. This was a forced labour for a nominal payment in kind. As it was an order of the king every one from all communities reported to the call, but Deena Bhadri did not attend, although they were available at the residence.

When they reached at the farm for harvest they found it difficult to do so because the farm was surrounded with the forest and it was very dark and they were afraid of wild animals. They felt the absence of Deena Bhadri badly because if they were available on the spot there was nothing to worry about animal. They might kill any animal in fun if at all it appeared before them, but who would do that in their absence, was the main anxiety for all assembled there. Every one looked pale and brightened but the work could not be undertaken.

The palace of Kanak Singh was at a very short distance from the place, where the labourers were sitting. Seeing them not working the two sisters Jadua and Bachua informed about this to Kanak Singh. He lost no time to reach there and asked the labaourers the reason for not working. They explained their fear for wild animal and requested the king to persuade Deena Bhadri to report on duty, only then they would be carefree to work.The king told them to stay their as he was going to call them soon.

On reaching at the house of Deena Bhadri, Kanak Singh saw their mother and told her to inform her sons that he was waiting for them outside. Deena Bhadri told their mother to tell the king that they were not there the king started scolding and abusing her as she told that her two sons were not available there. Listening to the abuses of the king Bhadri asked for the permission from his elder brother Deena to kill Singh for the insult of mother and when allowed attacked the king to kill him, but the mother intervened and protected the king from the death drap. Insulted and injured the king reached his place when his two sisters and others massaged him with oil and consoled by promising to get killed the two brothers by any means. Now the two sisters of the king were restless to find out a man who could kill Deena Bhadri. They tried their best by the magical power to appease all the Gods one by one to invoke to kill the two brothers, but all of them refused them, as they considered this task very risky. At last they came to know that Raja Salhesh a more powerful man of the Dusadh caste was capable to kill them. The two sisters approached Salhesh for the same. Raja Salhesh agreed to kill them on the condition that the responsibility of appearing them after death would rest on them and this was accepted by them. Raja Salhesh was an incarnation and possessed several supernatural powers.

On night Salhesh managed in a dream to suggest Deena Bhadri that a forest of Mahua near Katiadhar was full of games were hunging could be a pleasure. The day following they decided to go for a hunt that side. The mother objected to this because only the other day they had quarrel with the king. The two brothers were adament to go for the game, the mother asked them to await for their maternal uncle Barahan Singh whom she would fetch shortly. The two brothers liked the proposed of mother to enjoy the company of Mama in the game. They waited for a while for them to come back, but as there was some delay in their return Deena Bhadri left for the forest.

When they reached the forest, to their surprise there was not a single game worth the name. Then Bhadri climbed an Ashok tree to discover whether there were any game. He saw a deer which managed to walk on only one leg. They decided to kill this very deer. When they approached it Bhadri took out his bow and arrow and fired several aiming at the deer, but to their surprise none of these hit it as all of them glided. Thus, infuriated at the failure both Deena and Bhadri took out the suginia arrows which were infailable. When they fired suginia arrows which hit the deer it converted itself into a ferocious tigress which stood on the two back feet and started roaring out of anger. This was a novel situation but they did not lose heart and attacked the tigress with full strength. They fought for seven days without any food and rest. On the seventh day the tigress delivered five more cubs which suddenly grew as grown up tigers. Seeing this, they felt some foul-play with them and knew that the end of life was very near. Therefore, they decided to put an end of this life by the yogic method.

They slept on the earth head towards north and feet towards south and told the tigers not to touch them or they would create Chavoc for all. Thus, they died in the posture of sleep. Thereafter the tigers also disappeared only the old tigress was fanning them with neem leaves. Deena Bhadri told their parents in the dream about their death and also described about the place where their dead bodies were laying which were to be burnt in the proper way. They gave a message for the Dhamin (magician) that if on the eighth day of their death their spirit was not properly appeased, they will kill all the members of entire Dhamin families. The parents rushed towards the forest the next morning and were so sorry to find out their two darling sons dead. They were creamated in the forest with help of Barhan Rishi and others. So many super natural phenomena happened one after another by which people could believe in their power even after death. Some small quantity of rice was cooked which turned into heap of boild rice. Similarly, meat and other vegetables also increased many times than were arranged. Hundreds of castemen were fed on the occasion of Bhoj but only a portion of the cooked food were consumed, thus there were huge left over which were burried later on.

Kanak Singh started torturing the old parents of Deena Bhadri after their death. He told them to clean the dense forest of ten Kathas of land within one day or they would be punished. When the old parents reached at the place of work Deena Bhadri met the old parents in guise of cowherds and cleaned the forest for the parent in no time.

On another occasion Kanak Singh asked Kalu Sardar to fence a piece of land with trees and make gates on both sides. He wanted this for a gathering of his magicians. Deena Bhadri made all these in disguise and ultimately killed all the magicians, kanak and his two sisters Jadua and Bachua.

There are other stories also which speak of goodness and greatness of Deena Bhadri but common element in all of them is that they were twin brothers who possessed supernatural power of granting life to dead, punished the wicked people how so ever powerful one night be, helped the poor and needy men. Women who had painful delivery if prayed for help to Deena-Bhadri they were also attended to and normal child birth without pain was assured of their mercy.

The Mushars have strong faith in the helpful and kind attitude of Deena Bhadri for all of them and always protect them from the evils of ghost, witches and several other malevolent spirits which roam about every where and is harmful for them. The Musahars are in habit in reciting the names of Deena Bhadri whenever they need their help and it is commonly believed that they are omnipresent.

Deena-Bhadri Puja

The Musahars by tradition maintain a sacred centre-Deena Bhadri Sthan. In appearance it possesses a small raised platform made of bricks or earth. Two big bamboos are fixed in the centre of the platform. This place itself is insignia of the fact that the Musahar must be living in the nearby houses.

It is very clear from the above paragraph that Deena bhadri are village gods and as such they are enshrined at a public place open for all the musahars. The Puja of Deena Bhadri is also arranged on the community level where a sacred specialist of the community known as the Bhagat worships them on behalf of all of them. Ashadhi Puja is the main annual community worship as per detail given below:

Ashadhi Puja of Deena Bhadri is celebrated on the eve of Ashadh Purnima. Several days before this date all the old Musahars of the village will assemble at a place to discuss the various aspects of the Puja. This has to be financed by the subscription from each Musahar family. The Chharidar fixed the amount of subscription and may collect it himself or through any agent. He assigns other duties related to the puja to other members of the community. The main material for the puja are bamboo, winnowing fan, Kalsa, Dhupchi, rope of kusa grass, Mango twig, bow and arrow, Hanuman Danta, mustard oil, Dhuban, choora, curd, sugar, arwa, rice, kele, long, elaychi, pakwan and some other sweet, lot of red and yellow flowers, belpatta and tulsidal etc.

On the day of Ashadhi Puja the Bhagat has to observe fast from the dawn to dusk. On the day of Puja two big bambooes which should be quite erect are brought while bringing them it is observed that the bambooes should not touch the ground, because those are cleaned in a tank. The platform on which the bambooes are to be errected is kept ready by applying cowdung plastering when the bambooes reach on the spot of puja the old ones which were planted last year have to be uprooted before the new ones are planted. Some paddy one bow a few flowers etc. are tied at the top of one of the bambooes in another bamboo a piece of red saloo cloth often with the image of lord Hanuman is fixed on the top after which two holes are dug on the platform in which the two big bamboo poles are planted. Now the old poles which are uprooted are turn into pieces to be used as fuel for cooking the pudding for the puja.

After the Dhwaja of Deena Bhadri is planted, once again the platform is cleaned with cowdung paste. Several Diyas have to be lit which are placed on all the four sides of the platform. Gangajal is sprinkled, there after other materials of the puja 108 flowers along with Tulsidal and Vermillion, Choradahi, pan and several other materials are kept on the platform. The environment is charged with the loud beating of drum and piphe. Everyone is kept busy with doing something. Now the Bhagat starts puja. He will whisper something to self and will offer a few flowers and other material one by one. He will lose temper on his assistants and other organisers for a trifling fault and every one has to be very cautious at the time of puja. Situation becomes very tense when persons infected with witches and spirits are treated by the Bhagat towards the close of function in the late evening. Sometimes there is a long dialogue between the Bhagat and spirit on the terms and conditions which if agreed upon, the spirit may desert the infested person. Towards the close of function which takes about three hours time the prasad is distributed among all present there. It has been mentioned earlier that kheer and puree besides other sweets as laddu, pera are offered as prasad. One thing very peculiar about this worship is that, only male members remain present on the spot of puja and females are not allowed entry. Prasad is also a taboo for them. It appears that Deena Bhadri hated the two wicked sisters of Kanak Singh who ultimately hatched their murder also, therefore females are kept at a distance from them. It was reported that the Musahar female could recite their names when they were in trouble but could not pray or worship them for the reason not known to them.

Thus, it is clear from the perusal of a few foregoing pages that the Musahar is a sheduled caste found in a very good number in the north Bihar. They are very primitive people. Economically, Politically and educationally they are much behind other people of the locality.

The Brahmin is the dominant caste of most of these areas. The Musahars religious life is a bit complex. They believe in two sets of Gods and spirits. The first set is of the upper caste like Ram, Shiva, Durga etc, the Musahars pay due respect to them. The second set is of the deities of the musahar community of which Deena Bhadri is the supreme. They are great devotees of him and pay maximum respect for him. They feel that they are always protected by their supreme God who is omnipresent.

7

ECONOMIC PROBLEMS OF THE SCHEDULED CASTES OF BIHAR

The term "Scheduled Caste" is not only the name of particular caste, but it is a group of such people from among the untouchables who have been declared by the President of India ás Scheduled Castes. Tracing the origin of the scheduled castes one has to go back to the origin of caste itself. In the Vedic period also these people existed under the name of the Shudra. The term Shudra was one of the divisions of the Varnashrama Dharma among the four Varnas-Brahman, Kshatriya, Vaishya and Shudra. It appears that perhaps in those days there was no superiority and inferiority feelings to the extent it was treated latter on, but all the Varnas were interdependent to each other. "The great crusader, Mahatma Gandhi, in a bid to end the social stigma attached with them, termed them as Harijan (son of God) and as such he tried to bring them at par of the clean castes, otherwise they were unsocial being in the eyes of other superior castes.

Sociologists and social anthropologists, who have analysed the system of caste stratification in relation to the scheduled castes have lent support to the view that untouchability is a unique and added dimension of the caste system. The Hindu Caste Society has been characterised by the principles of purity and pollution, the determination of social rank by ritual criteria and by endogamy in the matters of marriage. In view of these considerations the problem of Independent India have been two fold: firstly, to remove social inequality to ensure higher place to the so-called untouchables and secondly, to forge their emotional and economic integration with mainstream of Indian society.

The Caste System is said to have played a significant part in the survival of Hindu culture in the face of numerous political conquests during the last several centuries. But at the same time it has also been responsible for promoting many a fissiparous tendencies in societies and perpetuation of untouchability in one of them. As regards the meaning of untouchability it can be understood from two angles: (i) the stigma attached to certain people because of the ceremonial pollution they allegedly convey and (ii) the set practice engaged in by the rest of the society to protect itself from the pollution conveyed by untouchables. The disabilities of the untouchable Hindu castes fall under religious, social and civil areas. The untouchable were denied access to temple and the services of the Brahmins and such other artisan castes of Hindu society and were prohibited entry to schools, roads and wells used by the high castes. In certain parts of India specially in south India even seeing them was considered a sin. Ambedkar has rightly observed. "This type of untouchability among Hindu, stand in a class by itself.... there is nothing which can make the untouchables pure.......they are born impure, they are impure while they live, they have the death of the impure and they give birth to children who are born with the stigma of untouchability affixed to them".

According to 1981 census the population of the Scheduled Castes comes to be million which constitutes 14.6 percent of the total Indian population. While the Scheduled Castes are distributed in the different states of our country a little more than half of the number of the Scheduled castes live in four states namely, Uttar Pradesh (48.5 million), Bihar (7.9 million), West Bengal (8.8 million) and Tamil Nadu (7.3 million).

These Scheduled Castes are mainly landless agricultural labourers and are exclusively dependent upon the landed high castes of their respective villages for their livelihood. Some of the scheduled castes however, are dependent on some specialised occupation like tanning and shoemaking, toddy trapping, fish catching, basketry, scavanging etc. Educationally they continue to be backwards as according to the census of 1961, 90 percent of them are still completely illiterate and only 8 percent of them are literate without any educational level. There are only 2.5 percent scheduled caste population who received primary or junior basic education and only 0.25 percent could reach educational standard of Matriculation or above.

The enactment of untouchability offensive Act of 1955 makes any type of discrimination against the Scheduled Castes in public place etc.

as punishable. According to this Act, the persons practising any type of untouchability prohibiting a member of the scheduled Caste to use the public place of worship or public restaurants, shops, hostels etc. would be punished. In view of these constitutional provisions, legal safeguards and plans of economic development there is considerable progress in raising the social and economic status of the Scheduled Castes. However, in the light of the recent researches among the scheduled castes of the Magahi and the tribal areas of Bihar certain phenomena deserve special consideration.

Despite the constitutional safeguard given to the members of the scheduled castes, the desired results to ensure their rise in the social scale and integration with the mainstream of Hindu society have not been achieved.Their economic, educational and general style of life remain deplorable.

Constitutionally the Scheduled Castes have been tagged with the Scheduled tribes, but to our mind, it is an inappropriate approach to lump together the problems of the Scheduled castes and the Scheduled tribes under one administrative machinery because of the differences in ecological, economic and cultural problems.

Again the term Scheduled Caste has been used as a blanket term to indicate a long list of backward castes though they suffer from distinct type of social disabilities, economic problems, and face different socio-political problems. For example, the scheduled castes of Artisan group (Turi, Panswansi and Chamra) of Chotanagpur have different set of problems as compared to the landless agricultural labourer group of the scheduled castes (Dusadh and Musahar) of Magahi area.

The state of Bihar has 14 percent population of 21 different scheduled and this paper is based on the field work done in two of the four major cultural linguistic zones at Bihar namely, (1) The tribal Zone and (2) the Magahi Zone (Vidyarthi 1969, pp. 122-134).

II

The Scheduled Castes of the Tribal Zone: Although Chotanagpur is famous for the tribal population but it has some scheduled castes too.

The following are the districtwise figures of the scheduled castes as per census of 1961.

Table No. 1

Name of the District	Total population of S.C.
1. Palamau	308,051
2. Hazaribagh	300,647
3. Dhanbad	206,967
4. Ranchi	97,300
5. Singhbhum	60,925

Thus, to have a comparative picture of the problems of the scheduled castes of Magahi and tribal areas, 175 families of the scheduled castes of tribal areas were selected and the field work was done in 14 different village namely, Dunardega, Siladon, Manhu, Birhu, Gutijora, Ghaghara and the like, within the district of Ranchi. The scheduled castes covered in the survey are five; Bogta, Panswansi, Ghasi, Turi Mahli and Chamar. A sample of 175 families with a population of 862 souls were selected for study in depth, the break ups of which are as follows:

Table No. 2

Sl. No.	Name of the Scheduled Caste	Total no. of Families	Total population
1.	Bhogta	43	215
2.	Panswansi	33	163
3.	Ghasi	42	198
4.	Turi Mahli	51	235
5.	Chamar	6	51
	Total	175	862

These communities though lumped together as a scheduled castes, are different from each other in terms of their economic specialisation and cultural characteristics. Before we undertake a general discussion about their economic problems, a brief ethnographic details merit our attention.

Bhogta

According to the 1961 census the Bhogtas have a population of 87,733 out of which,19,851 live in the villages of Ranchi district. They are mostly cultivators but also supplement their living through work in fields and in factories.They are famous Chura (Parched rice makers. Risley has ranked the Bhogtas socially at par with the Bhuiyas and Kharwars. 83.72 percent of them have land and rest of 16.28 percent are landless. Agriculture is the chief occupation for 97.67 percent Bhogtas of the villages covered under this study.

Panswansi

The Panswansis are weaving castes. They weaver cloths for the use of local people. They can be placed under the artisan group. They were 14,767 at 1961 census. They are found mostly in Sadar and the Khunti sub-divisions of Ranchi district. Although 90.91 percent of them have some land only 27.27 percent of them have agriculture as their main occupation where as 60.61percent of them are still weavers. Their traditional occupation in this district is cotton weaving. But there has been a huge deviation from the traditional occupation as they have failed to compete with the mill made fine and cheap cotton goods.

Ghasi

The Ghasi of Chotanagpur are musicians. They beat Dhol, Dhak and drums and play on Sahnai on various magico religious functions and festivals like Chuathi and marriage which are performed by the members of other castes. They also are traditional fisher men. They catch fish with the help of Kumni, Jhimri, Kurwu and Jal (Net) and sell them at the hands of local people. In this way we can put them in both the groups of artisan and fishing community. They numbered 55,034 at 1961 census. Only 47.62 percent of them had some land in the sample villages and only 4.76 percent of them had agriculture as their main occupation. A vast majority of 90.48 percent of them had fishing and drum beating as their main occupation.

Turi Mahli

The Turi Mahlis are basket makers. They manufacture different kinds of things from bamboo for household usages. Mostly, the People buy baskets, winnowing fans, Dhak, bamboo umbrella etc. from the local Turi Mahlis. So these people can also be put in the artisan group. According to 1961 census the total population of Turi in Bihar was 90.436 . The field work data show that 66,67 percent of them have some land but not even one of them accept agriculture as their main occupation. 98.04 percent of them have basketry as their main occupation.

Chamar

The Chamars have the largest population among the scheduled castes. As per census of 1961 they have a total population of 1,895,179 distributed throughout the state, and there is no district or block where they are not to be found. In our sample, however, they are very inadequately represented in Chotanagpur. The Chamars are the leather workers. They sometimes tan leather and manufacture as well as repair chappal and shoes. Economically they are better off than other Scheduled Castes as 100 percent of them have some land in the sample villages. They have some business of shoe-making and tanning. They have the highest income among the Scheduled Castes and by and large they are not indebted.

Economy of the Scheduled Castes of Chotanagpur

In terms of their occupation and means of livelihood, the population of scheduled castes in Chotanagpur are dependent either on agriculture or on certain crafts. The following table 3, brings out the extent of their dependence on land or on craft.

Table No. 3

Major Economic Groups Family-wise

Caste	No. of household	Agriculture	Artisan	Fishing	Others
Bhogta	43	42	20	-	1
Panswansi	33	9	2	-	4
Ghasi (Also Drummer)	42	2	-	38	-
Turi Mahli	51	0	50	-	1
Chamar	6	0	6	-	-
Total	175	53	78	38	6

The people dependent on land have either land or are landless labourer. From the Table 4, it is clear that, in general, 72 percent of the scheduled caste have some landed property whereas 28 percent of them are completely landless. The caste-wise figure shows that all the Chamars have some land though the percentage of the sample is small and no conclusion should be drawn on this basis.

Table No. 4

Number and percentage of landed property family wise

Caste	Total No. of family	No. and % of house hold possessing land		No. and % of land less house hold	
		No.	%	No.	%
Bhogta	43	36	83.72	7	16.28
Panswansi	33	30	90.91	3	9.09
Ghasi	42	20	47.62	22	52.38
Turi	51	34	66.67	17	33.33
Mahli	6	6	100	-	-
Chamar					
Total	175	126	72	49	28

Social Disabilities

It has been mentioned earlier that the scheduled castes, in general, have suffered a lot due to the stigma of untouchability. In the tribal areas initially the scheduled castes were brought by the other upper castes to discharge the traditional service. It is said that the Panswansis had been associated by the Mundas since inception for weaving cloths for them. The Turi Mahlis had also been brought by the people of Chotanagpur. The Ghasis, the Chamars and the Bhogtas had been brought by the local Raja and Zamindars for their own purposes. As most of the scheduled castes of the area are artisans and have been rendering very useful services to the co-villagers, as the region has remained cut off from the main stream of Hinduism, they found better deal in the areas as compared to their counterpart in Magahi area. Again, after independence the scheduled castes were lumped up with the scheduled tribes of the same area of their welfare, each one tried to accomodate the other. Although inter dinning between the scheduled castes and the tribes has not yet come in practice, the tribal people are not so rigid in the exchange of greetings. Bidi Tambakoo and raw articles, as the clean castes of the Magahi area. In general in a tribal village, the Harijans have more common problems than a Hindu caste village, particularly dominated by the twice-born.

Thus, to sum up, the economic problems of the scheduled castes of tribal area present an optimistic picture as they do not suffer at the land of the landed aristocracy and supplement their economy with that of their specialised occupation.The scheduled castes in Bihar, however, by and large, are landless agricultural labourers. In the tribal areas a vast majority of 72 percent of them have landed property, 66 percent of them practise certain art and craft and decidedly are better off economically than the unskilled agricultural labourers of Magahi area. Since the population of the scheduled castes is less, and as they render useful services they are taken in high esteem by the tribal folk. The stigma of untouchability is thin, as such psychologically and socially also the Harijans of tribal area are much better off than that of Magahi and Maithili cultural zones.

As such it does not appear sound to compare the economic problems of the Harijans of Magahi zone with that of the tribal zone, and this is why the economic problems of the scheduled castes of the Magahi zone is dealt separately in a few foregoing pages.

III

The Scheduled Castes of Magahi Zone

It has been mentioned earlier that Magahi is a cultural linguistic zone in the State of Bihar comprising roughly of Patna, Gaya, Nawada and Nalanda districts where Magahi dialect is spoken. There is a huge concentration of scheduled caste population in these areas. According to 1961 census their population comes to be 474,501 and 895,022 in the districts of Patna and Gaya respectively.

In the Magahi area the field work was done in a few villages namely Meyar, Garor, Pilkhi, Barar, Nakpur and the like near Rajgir in Nalanda districts in which 240 families of Harijan were selected for the intensive study, the details of which are given in the following table :

Table No. 5

Sl. No.	Name of the Scheduled Caste	Total families	Total Population
1.	Musahar	75	295
2.	Chamar	75	356
3.	Rajwar	65	313
4.	Dusadh	25	93
	Total	240	1,057

Thus, the four scheduled castes mentioned above the major Harijans group of Bihar in general and the Magahi area in particular. Their total population castewise as per 1961 census is given in the following table:-

Table No. 6

Sl. No.	Name of the Scheduled caste	Total population in Bihar	Percentage of total population
1.	Chamar	1,895,179	29
2.	Dusadh	1,724,553	26.30
3.	Musahar	1,007,340	15.41
4.	Rajwar	1,55,174	2.37

The Scheduled Castes of this area are mainly landless agricultural labourers and are exclusively dependent upon the Koiri, the Kurmi and the Gwala who have landed property. Excepting a few families of the Chamars who have some land and also work on leather, all the other Harijan communities namely Dusadh, Musahar and Rajwar are, by and large, the agricultural labourers. The following is the detail of their classification based on the traditional occupation:

Table No. 7

Name of Caste	No. of house hold	Agricultural		Agricultural Labourers		Service		Leather work	
		No.	%	No.	%	No.	%	No.	%
Musahar	75	22	29.27	49	65.28	4	5.45	-	-
Chamar	75	22	29.27	41	55.87	1	1.33	10	13.53
Rajwar	65	4	6.53	60	91.93	1	1.54	-	-
Dusadh	25	4	12	21	84	1	4	-	-
Total	240	51	21.25	171	71.25	7	2.92	10	4.17

Thus, it is clear from the perusal of Table No. 7 that a vast majority of 71.25 percent of the total scheduled caste population of the Magahi area are completely agriculture labourers whereas only 21.25 percent and 4.17 percent of them are engaged in agriculture and leather work respectively. The occupational pattern of the scheduled caste of the tribal area was quite different because 66 percent of them belonged to the group of Artisan which were semi-skilled and self employed.

The extent of landlessness

India is mainly a country of villages. More than 80 percent of Indian population live in the villages. The villagers are mostly dependent upon agriculture for their livelihood, and the yield of land is the major source of their income. But hard is the luck of the scheduled caste folk who are mostly landless. Land although a free gift of nature has been gift of nature has been the most important factor of production and only a handful of upper caste people have monopoly over the cultivable land. The field work data from the Magahi area reveal that whereas only 20.21 percent villagers of Garor belonging to the upper castes are landless the percentage of landlessness among the scheduled caste goes upto 42.90 percent Similarly, in the village of Meyar only 4.5 percent of the villagers of the upper castes are landless whereas landlessness among the scheduled caste is 65.55 percent. A look into the following table may give the picture of the extent of landlessness and meagre possession of land among the scheduled caste.

Table No. 8

Name of Caste	No. of house hold	Landless		Below 1 Bigha		Quantity of land 1-10		Total landed property	
		No.	%	No.	%	No.	%	No.	%
Mushar	75	53	70.59	4	5.32	18	23.94	22	29.33
Chamar	75	36	47.88	16	21.28	23	30.59	39	52
Rajwar	65	54	82.62	6	9.18	5	7.65	11	16.92
Dusadh	25	9	36	13	52	3	12	16	64
Total	240	152	63..33	39	16.25	49	20.42	88	36.67

The sleepy extent of landlessness is clear from the perusal of the table mentioned above. A vast majority of 82.62 percent of Rajwar, 70.59 % of Musahar, 47.88 percent of Chamar. 36 percent of Dusadh, 63.33 percent of the scheduled caste in general of Magani area are completely landless. Even those who have some land it is meagre because 16.25 percent of them possess below one Bigha whereas only 20.42 percent of the possess between 1 to 10 Bighas. The case of Kajwar and Mosahar appears to be very hard as very few of them have some land worth the name.

A comparative picture of the possession of land and its quantity by the members of the upper and scheduled castes in the village of Garor under Nalanda district reveals that whereas 10.75 percent upper caste people have one Bigha of land, the percentage of the scheduled caste is 27.69 meaning thereby that more of the scheduled castes have less land. Again, the possession of 1 to 10 Bighas of land is held by 46.44 percent persons of the upper castes and only 25.88 percent of the scheduled castes. Similarly, 10.50 percent of the upper caste people are in the group possessing 11 to 100 Bighas of land, while not even a single family of the scheduled caste was reported in this group.

It has been mentioned earlier that there is landlessness even among the scheduled castes of tribal area. But here the extent of landlessness is alarming. Whereas only 28 percent scheduled castes of the tribal area are land less, here in the case of Magahi area, there are 63.33 percent scheduled castes having no land. Strangely although 72 percent scheduled castes of the tribal area have some land only 30.29 percent of them depend mainly on agriculture, whereas 66 of them have their own art and craft as the members of the Artisan group. Here in the case of Magahi area although only 36.67 percent of them have some land, a vast majority of 71.25 percent (excluding 21.25 percent engaged in agriculture) employed as agricultural labourers.

Economic Categories

It is evident from the preceeding pages that the scheduled castes of Magahi area are mainly engaged as agricultural labourers, though they may do several jobs, like agriculture, service, tanning of skin, basketry, collection of wood and herbs from the hills of Rajgir to supplement their economy. Agricultural labour is their main occupation since 71.25 percent of them are mainly dependent on it whereas only 21.25 percent 22.92 percent and 4.17 percent of them depend on agriculture, service and leather work respectively.

The caste-wise economic category indicates that only 29.27 percent Musahar have their main occupation as agriculture, whereas 65.28 percent of them are mainly agricultural labourers and only 5.45 percent are in services. Similarly, only 29.27 percent of Chamars depend on cultivation 55.87 percent on agricultural labour, 1.53 percent on the leather work, the age old traditional occupation of the caste. The Rajwars have the minimum percentage (6.53 percent) under cultivation, whereas 91.93 percent of them depend entirely on agricultural labour and only 1.54 percent are dependent on service. Like the Rajwar, the percentage of Dusadh for agriculture is very meagre (12 percent) whereas 84 percent of them are engaged as agricultural labourers and 4 percent in the service mainly of Choukidar (watchman).

Thus the scheduled castes as a whole of this area can be put into following four economic categories with their percentage:

1. Agricultural labour	71.25
2. Agriculture	21.25
3. Leather work	4.17
4. Service	2.92

Appointment of agricultural labourers and the mode of payment

Unlike the factory labour an agriculturer is appointed every day, only for that day, and generally for a piece of work to be finished within the limited time. They are paid in kind every day. In the Magahi area particularly in the sample villages the Koiri, the Kurmi and the Gowala are the cultivators who engage agricultural labourers.While engaging a labour the employer has preference for a young and energetic male who is not dull nor talkative only males are engaged for ploughing, swing and irrigating whereas for transplantation of the paddy seedlings which require bulk supply of labour and even the women are engaged. Similarly for harvesting all men, women and children can be engaged as a particular field has to be harvested fully by the evening hence no choice is left with the employer. Regarding the payment of wage the following categories are identified according to the amount of payment for the various works.

Nature of Work Done

Payment made

1. Ploughing, sowing or irrigating - 3 Seers (Kachchi) of grain, 3/4 for about 8 hours. Seer of Sattu (gram powder) and 1/8 seer of Chabana (fried gram and maize) as daily wage.
2. Transplantation of paddy - 5 Seers (Kachchi) of grains and 3/4 seedlings there is no fixed 4 seer of Sattu as daily wage hours, generally a particular field has to be transplanted in full.
3. Harvesting the crops Here, the payment is made on the basis of the work done. It is a labour contract where labourer is paid

one bundle of paddy harvested for every eleven to fifteen bundles (Anti) varying in the villages.

In addition to the wages mentioned above a few labourers who are attached with some fixed cultivator, more commonly for ploughing may get 10 to 15 Kathas of land to till and his master would not claim for and portion of the produce of the land. But then the labourer is obliged to seek the permission of his master to work in other's farms when the letter does not require him. Some occasional help from the master is expected in the event of marriage and death. But this attachment does not hold good only for the one labourer but for the entire family members, hence their mobility to work in others farm is restricted.

From the wage structure prevalent among the scheduled castes it is clear that they are paid very low. Again it is also clear that some elements of bonded labour is also prevalent. It has been mentioned earlier that the employers have a preference for young male labourer who should be hardy. The supply of labour is huge as 71.25 percent of them are landless agricultural labourers, and in this area there is practically no industry worth the name. Hence, the employers have choice, whereas the labours who have neither an organiséd labour market nor trade unionism among them nor patience to wait to bargain due to poverty, are forced to accept the terms dictated by the masters. Thus, except the four busy months of transplantation and harvest, when there is full employment of all the labourers, irrespective of the factor of age and sex, the period of eight months is very hard. Roughly only one adult male per family may get the job of a ploughman in these hard months. Others although able and willing to work remain unemployed for want of job opportunity. Thus, whereas in the average there are five members in a family there is only one person who gets about 4 seers of grain to maintain the family.

The Problem of seasonal unemployment leading to migration: As has been mentioned earlier the job opportunity is not uniform all the year round in the agricultural operations and these poor Harijans have no saving to struggle during the hard eight months of unemployment. This compels them to go out of the village. Those who are not fit or have some personal difficulty in going out engage themselves in some non-agricultural work like collection of fire wood, and herbs from the hills of Rajgir, fishing and rope making etc. A large number of them Migrate to work as casual labourers, collies, rickshaw pullers in the town of Rajgir. Some of them have gone to Calcutta to work as dock labourers whereas others go to the coal field areas. Some Rajwar and Dusadh young boys and girls go to Rajgir and serve in the hotels as servants and maid servants. But all of them normally come back by the time of harvest. This seasonal migration though by and large limited to young men alone has some very serious implications. Most of them fall ill due to inhospitable climatic condition of the places, particularly during rainy season. Sometimes their entire saving is stolen while they are out to work. The cases of fraud and of pickpocket at the time of return journey to village home are also very high.

Jajmani system and the problem of deviation from the Traditional Occupation

Just by the irony of luck only the Chamars out of the four scheduled castes selected from the Magahi area have Jajmani system for their service. Siva Ram Mochi, for example, has about twenty families attached with him for his service. Other castes namely, Dusadh, Mushar and Rajwar do not find place in the network of the Jajmani system. This makes them economically more insecure.

All the castes have their traditional occupations which are essentially hereditary in nature. For example, a Pasi is the toddy trappers and a Lohar is the ironsmith. One inherits not only the property of father but his trade also and normally there is a tendency of persistence in it. But owing to some pressure the scheduled castes under study have left their age old traditional occupation and have adopoted the new ones and this has been termed as "deviation from the traditional occupation". Such deviations from the traditional occupation of Musahar, Chamar, Rajwar and Dusadh come to the extent of 14.67 percent, 20 percent, 18.46 percent and 4 percent respectively. A large number of answansis have stopped the job of weaving. Similarly, the Chamar of Magahi area famous for the shoe-making have lost the trade as their technique was outdated and they could produce only shoes of old model which had no demand. Moreover, mill made shoes were durable and cheaper. Thus, even the artisan communities are losing their trade and this has added to the number of unemployed labourers. There are some who have left their traditional occupation which was an impediment to their absorption into the Hindu mainstream but then all of them could not succeed. Thus, they have lost their old traditional occupation and have gained none. All these have caused confusion in the social order and economic life.

The Problem of Indelatedness

The Scheduled Castes in general are indebted to the village Mahajans, ex-landlord and Sahukars. Thus, the common proverb that Indian peasants are born in debt, live in debt and die in debt, holds good with the Harijans too. But before anything is said about their indebtedness, a few facts about their meager income deserves to be mentioned. The survey of scheduled castes for the point of income group, indicates that they could be classified under the following categories :

Income groups (annual)	Percentage	Household
1. Below Rs. 500-3000	72.16	175
2. Below Rs. 3100-5000	23.90	57
3. Rs. 5100 and above	3.41	7

From the above chart, it is evident that 72.16 percent of the total families belong to the lowest income group of Rs. 500 to 30,000 annually. The medium income group of Rs. 3100-5000 annually have 23.90 percent families whereas only 3.41 of families belong to the group of Rs. 5100 and above. Hence, barring a few, most of them are economically handicapped and hence fall prey to indebtedness.

As regards the cause of indebtedness, special mention may be made of the (1) failure of crops, (2) to meet family obligations, (3) treatment of diseases and (4) such other reasons. Some of the most common causes for which they borrow are given in the following table along with the percentage of responses.

Table No. 9

Sl. No.	Purpose of borrowing	Percentage
1.	To fight the drought	35.72
2.	Festivals and social customs	20
3.	Treatment of disease	17.85
4.	To meet the marriage expense	15.72
5.	To purchase seed, fertilizer and agricultural implements	5.72
6.	To meet family expenses during the days of unemployment	0.71
7.	Miscellaneous purposes	4.28

Thus, it is clear from the table mentioned above that the poor Harijans borrow money mostly to fight the drought although drought is a natural calamity affecting every one within the area. It however affects the poor Harijan more than upper caste people as they do not posses the irrigation implements which are expensive. Hence, in the event if drought they have to hire it on a very high rent. It the drought is a very acute that affects the employment opportunities of the Harijans as the cultivators do not want to invest the little grain they have left with them. This situation becomes a matter of trial for the poor Harijans. A large number of them borrow to celebrate festivals, for the treatment and also for the marriage expenses. Thus, a perusal into the various purposes for loan received, reveals that more than 90 percent of loan is taken for economically non-productive purposes whereas only 5.72 percent of loan is taken for productive purpose as such the repayment of the debt becomes a difficult problem.

The Source of Loan

In the village of India there is no bank but the bankers in the villages are the Mahajans, the Indian Jews. They are engaged in money lending business, and charging as exorbitant rate of interest is the only motto with them. The minimum rate of interest is 25 percent in compound and for the maximum it is unlimited. They believe in the policy "once a debtor always a debtor" once an innocent Harijan goes in their clutch it is quite a difficult task to come out of it.

The field data regarding the extent of indebtedness indicate that 45.8 percent of the Harijans in general are indebted to the Mahajans. Their caste-wise distribution is given in the following table:

Table No. 10

Sl. No.	Caste	Household	Percentage
1.	Musahar	38	50.17
2.	Chamar	37	49.3
3.	Rajwar	25	38.5
4.	Dusadh	10	40.0

Repayment of Loan

It has been mentioned earlier that most of the loan is taken for non-productive purposes hence its repayment is a difficult problem. Since the rate of interest is exorbitant a debtor is always anxious to pay the interest because he knows it fully that the repayment of the principal amount is rather beyond his means.

The various sources for paying back the debt may be grouped into three categories and their wise percentages are given in Table No. 11:

Table No. 11

Sl. No.	Caste	Total household	In kind	From wage	From sale of land and ornaments
1.	Musahar	75	15.78	76.31	7.89
2.	Chamar	75	5.41	86.48	8.11
3.	Rajwar	65	24.0	72.0	4.0
4.	Dusadh	25	20.0	70.0	10.0
	Total	240	14.55	78.18	7.27

It is interesting to note as the agricultural labourers are paid poorly, only the 78.18 percent of loan is repaid in the shape of hard earned wages of the labour. The payment in "kind" includes repayment in crops mostly the paddy. The poor Labour saves some grains during the period of harvest when all of them get opportunity to work hard from dawn to dusk, and thus pay back the debt, and 14 percent of debt is paid back from this source. It has been mentioned at several places that most of the Harijans are landless, even in some hard case, when they fail to tolerate the pressure of the Mahajans any more, they pay back 7.27 percent of loan by selling the meager land and ornaments.

Observations

The Scheduled castes in general are landless agricultural labourers. Economically, the scheduled castes of Chotanagpur are better off than those of Magahi area, because a vast majority of them are self employed as Artisan whereas more than 70 percent of their counterpart in Magahi area fall back on the landed upper caste people. The economic life of these people is most insecured because of their casual appointment and daily payment. The wages paid to them is meager and certainly insufficient for the proper living. Very few of them are absorbed in the Jajmani system. The social stigma of untouchability attached with them still persists in the Magahi area, that prevents them in getting many household jobs in the family of upper castes. The seasonal unemployment compels many youths to migrate elsewhere but that too proves harmful. The natural calamity in form of drought and famine always lurk like the sword of Democes. The cases of deviation from the traditional occupation do occur among them which has been responsible for the transition hence instability.

Landless as they are, and a meager wage that they set, they do not have saving worth the name. Hence, in case of difficulties they go to the village Mahajans for loans. About 45 percent of them are badly indebted to the village Mahajans. They have to pay an exhorbitant rate of interest. The cunning and merciless money lenders sometimes compel them to sell the small pieces of land if one has. A debtor has to face the humiliation of the Mahajan, and leads a demorlised life. Their standard of living is very very low, hence they fail to aspire for any higher status.

The task is stupendous. Much efforts have been done since Gandhiji drew attention of the nation. Many legislations have been adopted. A fresh effort has been initiated under the 20-point programmes and the State Govt have done men's service for them very recently by salvaging them from the clutches of the villages, Mahajans the Indian Jews. It is hoped that the Harijan of the great crusader Mahatma Gandhi will not lag behind any more, if time bound programmes are intensified.

8

PROBLEMS AND PROSPECTS OF SCHEDULED CASTES OF BIHAR

The Scheduled castes are those people who belong to the last Varna namely, the Shudra and Avarnas include many caste groups, having a total population of about eight million in Bihar, which have suffered social and economic disabilities and inequality since the ages. The concept of pollution was attached to them and they were treated as untouchable castes. Late Mahatma Gandhi called them Harijan which means people of God. Lateron the name Harijan was also not only disliked but was also hated and opposed by the untouchables. As a result it was duly replaced by the term scheduled castes in 1933 and it continuous to be used so in government records and circulars even today.

As has been mentioned earlier, the scheduled castes are bcackward socially and economically.Their backwardness is perhaps the root of all problems from which they have been suffering from ages.To discuss in detail about all their problems may not be possible here within such a short span of time but certainly I would like to discuss their major problems which if solved may give them some immediate relief. Landlessness is the most serious problem suffered by them. By and large the scheduled castes comprise the land of landless agricultural labour. They have no land to till even their huts in which they live stand on the plot of some ex-landlord or Mahajan who would demand labour in their farm. They work as share cropper or sajha on the land of upper caste people. But the type of land offered to them this purpose is not good, As has been told above that saheduled castes are in a particularly weak situation. Typically they are agricultural labourers. Others depend on small and marginal farming, fishing and other low-income occupations like basketing. Scavenging and other leather work. They own very small assets. Almost all of them are below the poverty line in the economic status. A national survey has revealed that 66 percent of the bonded labourers in the country belong to the scheduled castes. This type of abject poverty compels them to work as casual agricultural labourers in others farms. Indian agricultural labourers are the worst paid. Their lot is most pitiable they do not have organised market nor do they have a labour guild hence they are exploited every where. The wage paid to them is hardly enough to feed once a day.

Another serious problem from which the members of Scheduled castes suffer is the problem of untouchability and stigmatisation. Untouchability in India is intimately and organically associated with the institution of caste. Its rigid form is logical outcome of a peculiar notion of pollution sanctified by religion and codified by the Brahminical discriminative laws. The practise of untouchability has various forms each of which is inhuman, irrelevent and barbaric. Ambedkar has rightly observed 'This type of untouchability among Hindus stands in a class by itself. There is nothing which can make the untouchables pure....., they are born impure, they are impure while they live, they have the death of the impure, and they give birth to children who are born with the stigma of untouchability affixed on them. Social disability is a unique problem for the Harijan of India in general and Bihar in particular. Disability as a batter of fact, is the product of untouchability and manifested through caste interaction. The disabilities occur only in specific social situation created invariably by two or more groups from both clean and untouchable castes. For instance, in Bihar, there are people who would nor accept water from the hands of Harijans for fear of being polluted. For this reason some of them are deprived of earning their livelihood in some private sphere of interaction. Thus, very limited number of professions and occupation are accessible to them. At some places, similarly these people are prohibited from use of any utensil in a restaurant, hotel or Dharmashala. They are not permitted to approach any house owned by the member of upper caste. Any attempt to develop self respect by them is strictly discouraged by the clean caste people, assuming decent names or even donning dress after the high caste manner is deemed to be an affront to the upper caste. In the sphere of religion also they have to play very limited role at village level, In school also the Harijan children cannot get respite from such disabilities. They have been given to believe that these social handicaps are just as natural as any other daily routine. Even hospital treatment given to them is discriminatory. A notion is common among the upper caste about the intellectual inferiority of the Harijan hence they do not get justice for jobs so there are many kinds of socio-economic disabilities as it is evident from the Harijan grocer or owner of a hostel not finding clean caste patronage.

Thus, demoralised by the inhuman treatment given to the members of scheduled castes the upper caste people would not allow them to live even the sub-human life. They have to suffer from various types of exploitation and atrocities. The State of Bihar is notoriously in famous for all these evils. A look on any newspaper captures on eyes on the news published about the murder, burning, beating and several other tortures given to the scheduled castes. Carrages of Belchi, Pipra, parasbigha and the recent one of Arbal are some of the worst examples when scheduled castes men were surrounded by the vested interest, their houses were set ablaze, and when the inmates needed shelter, help and mercy. They were fired from guns and both wounded as well dead were thrown into the fire. These are very sad, shameful, cruel and unfortunate examples of the atrocities on the scheduled castes of Bihar.

Exploitation of the scheduled castes is very common and in view of the atrocities of serious type committed on them they have developed immunity and a sense of tolerance against this seldom a scavenger refuses to carry the head load of night soil in rural areas. Similarly, they are compled to carry on all the dirty indignified, inhygienic and profane duties without sufficient and proper reward there of. The evil practice of their being untouchable, unseenable, unapproachable and stigma of their being polluted, profane and inauspicious keeps them in the inhospitable and damp slums away from the main village. Naturally they become the first victim of epidemic, flood and fire devastation.

The evil practices of Begar, bonded labour, child labour are still prevalent in the villages and the scheduled caste men are the most exploited in all these deals. If they need loan, they have to pay an exorbitant rate of interest. If they fail to return, the moneylender may confiscate his little belonging and may best him. If they raise their voice in protest they are blended as naxalite and are thus implicated in several criminal cases.

The problems of scheduled castes have always been a matter of concern for the govts. social workers and other. After India won Independence there has been definite and consistent efforts by the Govts. to solve the problems of scheduled castes. Several legislations have come into effect to put an end to the evil practices of untouchability, bonded labour and child labour in a bid to give land to them the ceiling surplus land, the land earned through Bhoodan and the gair majaurwa lands have been distributed among them similarly they have been given the benefit of minimum wage for agricultural labour and they have been freed from their debts, as well. But the constitutional provisions for the protection and betterment of scheduled castes have mostly been a paper work their economic condition in so poor they are not in a mood to listen to all these which cannot give them breed to eat, roof over head, and protection from the musclemen of ex-landlords. If we sincerely wish them flourish, they have to be assimilated into the mainstream of popular Hinduism of India.

9

PROBLEMS OF HARIJAN CHILD LABOURERS AND THEIR WELFARE NEEDS IN BIHAR

It is difficult to pick up a newspaper or magazine today without finding some reference to the problems of child. Among the problems which often captures our attention the problems of child labour, child beggar, child kidnapping for ransom, child drug addiction, child abuse, smuggling of child to the Arabian countries for camel race and the like are very common.

All the problems enlisted above are serious, but to me, the problems of child labourer is general and those of the Harijan child labourers in particular are dangerously serious because whereas other problems are by and large taken as illegal, problems of Harijan child labourer which are also illegal in nature, have been accepted as a normal phenomenon in our society. For example, when a child is kidnapped, a F.I.R. is booked, but when a child is employed in a carpet factory or Bidi making trade no such case is booked, becaused, because this happens with the consent of the parents and more commonly the parents themself bring the children for jobs. Therefore, the study of the problems of these unfortunate Harijans children is more urgent and important.

It was 28th Oct 1990 when I read an article entitled "Swept under the carpet" published in the " Times of India," New Delhi. Dated Oct. 28, 90 by one Mr. Sumir Lal who had visited the carpet centres of Mirzapur Bhadohi. I was moved to read the inhuman condition in which the Harijan kids were working. I quote the abstract of the article "Swami Agnivesh's call to the international market to boycott carpets woven by children has reawakened the controversy on child labour. The

Governments concerns seems to be weighed more in favour of commerce than the overworked, underpaid, exploited kids".

The central theme of this paper is a case study of Mahendra, a 12 years old Harijan boy of Saharsa in Bihar, who works with four other boys from his home district for one Deonath Yadav, owns two looms which he operates in his house in Barasta village near Bhadohi in U.P. Mahendra is one of the thousand of children (one estimate puts their number to five lakhs) who works all through the day on looms scattered in numerous villages of the famous Mirzapur Bhadohi carpet weaving belt.

The employment of child labour below 14 years in the process of carpet weaving has been prohibited by law, cut the children of prohibited age group are mostly employed for the carpet weaving because they work continuously for the whole day ungrudgingly without a demand for the rest. The children are best suited for this trade because only a child's slender fingers can create knots of extreme intricacy and fineness, which determine a carpets' quality and there is that telling example of Iran which lost its premier position in the world carpet industry in the mid 70s when the then Shah, in an attempt to modernise the carpet industry, liberated thousands of child weavers and sent them to school.

The employers of these child labour believe that their parents should be obliged to them because they feed them failing which they may starve. What would have been their lot is a matter of debate, but the condition in which they have to work is far from being satisfactory and I quote from the same paper. The work condition of the thousands of children who operate the looms in the surrounding villages to put it mildly, are abominable. The boys sit in the dark staffy rooms with their legs dangling in the dank mud put in which the loom is anchored. They eat and sleep in the same rooms. There is no fresh air, and it does not require a laboratory test to sense the omnipresence of wool pluff. "The boys remain in a single position for hours on end shoulders and back hunched over the looms, their eyes wide in the dark. While their adroit fingers weave knots of intricate designs at an amazing speed. In fact, it is because of their slender and nimble fingers that children are employed on looms".

Brick Kiln is another industry in which the Harijan child labourers are engaged for various jobs. The brick layers exploit them in various ways. They are not paid properly nor behaved well. Very often the Harijan girls kept for cooking for the manager and other staff of the kiln are sexually exploited. The cases of abortion and suicide by these girls of tender age is very high.

Similarly, the condition of Harijan child labour employed in private open mines and quarry, tea gardens, plantain gardens, hotels, civil construction work and cow herd boy is far from being satisfactory. They are every where over worked and underpaid, exploited and illtreated, and forced to live a sub-human life.

The problems of child labour and their rehabilitation is a very deep rooted and multifaced. Most of the Harijan children turn up for job because their parents have been squeezed out of agricultural holdings or have been displaced by some development projects, for example, 318 Harijan families were displaced under Kiul Dam Project at Garhi in the district of Monghyr, Bihar. As many 262 Chamars, 35 Turi, 8 Musahar and 13 other Harijans were uprooted in this scheme in which a total area of 2856.95 acres of land was acquired. These poor Harijans were alloted some Gair Mazarua and barren land which were not cultivable in addition to some cash compensation.

I consider Bihar a very proper place for this study because Bihar is the third largest state in the Harijan population. According to census of India 1981, it has a total Harijan population of 10,142 ,468 which is 14.51 percent of the total population of the state. Although the Harijans are evenly distributed in all the districts, their percentage is large in northern Bihar than in South Bihar.

Under articles 34(i) and 342 (i) of the constitution of India the castes or tribes to be treated as scheduled castes or scheduled tribes for a particular state are specified by a public notification by the President of India. In Bihar 23 such lower caste Harijans have been listed as the scheduled castes.

The factor of caste has always been important in India, but it has become very important after its independence in 1947 and for an underdeveloped state like Bihar, recently this factor has become perhaps the most important. Keeping this in view, social and ethinic group composition in Bihar has been attempted through the following chart:

	Category	Total Percentage
1.	Upper Caste	12.7
2.	Backward Classes	34.4
3.	Other Shudras	14.6
4.	Muslims	12.2
5.	Scheduled Castes	14.5
6.	Scheduled Tribes	8.9
7.	Bengalis and Others	2.7
		100

Marijan Child Labour Defined

It is vivid from the perusal of the chart of the population composition of Bihar, mentioned above, that in all, there are 29.1 percent Shudras (15.5 % scheduled castes + 14.6 % other Shudras). But only 14.5 percent have been put under reservation and they get the benefit of the scheduled castes. As per constitutional provisions this population gets special treatment in every walk of life. There are only 23 such communities in the state of Bihar. These people were addressed to as "unclean castes", "Exterior castes", "depressed classes", "Chandala", "patitas," "Shudras" and the like. The term Harijan was an award to them by late Mahatma Gandhi, father of the nation to these downtrodden. Now, even the term Harijan, given to them has not been liked by many scheduled castes officials working in government offices. As D. Keer has said that Dr. Ambedkar, whose followers resented the term "Harijan" on being challenged to suggest as better term failed to do so.

The Harijans of Bihar are by and large landless agricultural labourers. Others depending on share cropping, small and marginal farming, fishing and other low income occupations like basketing, scavenging and leather work etc. They own very small assets. Almost all of them are below the poverty line in their economic status. A national survey has revealed that 66 percent of the bonded labourers of the country belong to Harijan community. Further, they have been subjected to various socio-economic disabilities like untouchability, unseenability, profanity and several other stigma of being liar and thief.

After a brief Introduction of the Harijans given above, the term child labour has also to be introduced. It is true that labour is the most active agent of production. Nothing can be produced in want of this. This is an era of technology and everywhere people talk about developed and modern technology but ultimately everything depends upon the human factor, and even the best technology can not replace it. I am tempted to quote late Pt. Jawahar Lal Nehru in this regard who observed "it is all very important and we must have them, but ultimately, of course, it is human being that counts, well, he counts much more as a child than as a grown up".

When we talk of child labour we have to define child labour first. Legally "child means a person who has not completed his fourteenth year of age", reference of this occurs in the constitution of India Article. 25 which reads "No child below the age of fourteen years shall be employed to work in any factory or mine or engaged any other hazardous employment". Thus, it is vivid that the framers of constitution regarded a labour upto the age of fourteen years as a child labour who were prohibited for certain difficult and hazardous jobs.

If we look at the age wise population composition of India in the census of 1981 we find that the population of the age group 1 to 14 years comes to 39.5 percent of the total population of India. The percentage of Harijan population in the same age group many be tentatively the same. We are more concerned about the Harijan population of Bihar for the present study. It has been mentioned in the very beginning that Bihar houses 10,142,468 Harijans as enumerated in 1981 census out of which the population of children upto the age of 14 years is 42,250,86. But this entire population can not be regarded as the labour force because normally a child upto four years is not able to do much even when the economic condition of the family does not spare it. It appears reasonable therefore to omit the age group 0-4 from the stock of labour force. The total population of the Harijan children upto 4 years is 14.12.192 if this is omitted the rest of 28,12,866 children will be the actual Harijan children labour force of 5 to 14 years of age. Thus the present study which is exploratory in nature aims at investigating, understanding and analysing the problems of these masses of more than 28 lakh unfortunate Harijan child labour of Bihar.

Besides a general survey of the nature and causes of Harijan children opting for working as labourers in various jobs. This will cover the nature and type of work for which they are engaged, the treatment they receive from their respective employer and the wage they are paid. The condition of the place one has to work and securities that are given to them. This will also cover aspects of joys and sorrows of child labour. Their problems and solution. Further to understand their problems in totality, there are several questions to be answered in this connection.

1. The first being why the Harijan children opt to labour during the tender years of childhood, when other children of this age group go to school. To answer this simple question one has to consider so many things. The economic condition of their parents, their family composition and total number of working person per family.

2. Second to assess the magnitude of poverty which is the root of this evil practice. It is known about the Harijans of Bihar that they are by and large landless agricultural labour having no or very little property. Normally, there are two adult persons in a nuclear family one male who is normally father and a female who is mother and their several unmarried children. The housewife is kept busy for child care, cooking, husking and collect fire-wood and looking after so many domestic jobs. The only adult male member has some chance of engagement as a daily casual labour for some agricultural operations. The wage which is normally in kind is not more than 3 to 4 kg of raw paddy or any other grain. Thus, the economic condition of an average family which has to survive on 3 to kg of raw grain per day is a thing to be imagined, unearning children are burden on the family. Hence, they have to labour anywhere for their bare survival. Their parents are not in a position to feed them and send them to school for education.

3. It is necessary to mention here that only 10.40 percent Harijan of Bihar are literate, hence their mental level and level of aspiration does not go beyond food and some clothes. Seldon they are serious about education and health of their children. All these they consider the play of fortune.

4. There are certain constitutional provisions to protect the child labour from certain hazardous jobs. To this effect an Act to prohibit the engagement of children in certain employments and to regulate the conditions of work of children in certain other employments were enacted by the Indian Parliament and received the assent of the President on December 23,1986 as "The Child Labour (Prohibition and Regulations) Act, 1986. The perusal of the said Act reveals that child labour have been prohibited against employment in certain occupations and processes which are given below in two parts :

Parts - A

Any occupation connected with :

i. Transport of passengers, goods or mails by railways.

ii. Cinder picking, cleaning of an ash pit or building operation in the railway premises.

iii. Work in a certain establishment to a railway station, involving the movement of a vendor or any other employee of the establishment from one platform to another or into or out of moving train.

iv. Work relating to the construction of a railway station or with any other work where such work is done in close proximity to or between the railway lines.

Part-B

Process

1. Bidi-making
2. Carpet weaving
3. Cement manufacture
4. Cloth printing, dying and weaving
5. Manufacture of matches, explosive and fire works
6. Mica cutting and splitting
7. Shellac manufacture
8. Soap manufacture
9. Tanning
10. Wool cleaning, and
11. Building and construction industry

Thus, from the perusal of the provisions of the Child Labour Act of 1986 it is clear that children have been prohibited to work in most of the trades. To study as to how far these provisions are operative in the actual life.

5. To examine the various welfare schemes available for the child labour and their efficacy to solve their problems.
6. To study in depth the cases of exploitation and atrocities on the child labour.
7. It appears that child labourers are not aware of the constitutional safeguard given to them.

To try to assess their awareness in this regard.

To examine the welfare needs of the Harijan child labourers. Very often the felt needs of the persons under review are ignored and ambitious schemes are adopted of their welfare. In most cases such schemes fail for want of public support. If necessary this study may suggest diversification of the welfare schemes aimed at ameliorating their overall socio-economic conditions better compulsory health and hygine and education for all the Harijan children.

It is that right from the UNICEF to the municipality of a small town are busy with innumerable schemes of child welfare, but their has been hardly any real development among the Harijans child labourers of Bihar. The conditions of the slum dwellers Harijan child labours are still worse. Govt. is trying best for their upliftment but this can be possible only with the help of all who live on the sacred land of Buddha and Mahavir.

10

SOCIO-ECONOMIC DISABILITIES OF THE HARIJANS OF MITHILA

INTRODUCTION

In the structure of Indian society, caste is of vital consideration and of immense importance and interest, not only for the sociologists and social anthropologists, but also for the majority of the Hindus, and to a smaller degree to the Muslims and the Christians, most of whom being converts from Hinduism, have not been able to get rid of this age old customs. The caste system is said to have played a significant role in the survival of the Hindu culture in the face of the numerous political conquests during the last several centuries. But at the same time it has been responsible for promoting many a fissiparous tendency in society and perpetuation of untouchability and several other socio-economic disabilities associated with the Harijan communities are some of them.

Tracing the origin of Harijan or the scheduled castes we have to go back to the origin of caste itself. According to the traditional theory of Varna, the shudras were supposed to have sprung from the feet of the creator and the scheduled castes of to-day are said to belong to the Shudra Varna. They have been addressed to be several derogatory terms like the Patitas, the Chandalas, the Untyaja, Achhoota etc. Since the enactment of Government of India Act of 1935 they have been consistently referred to as the Scheduled Castes.

The term 'Harijan' was coined by the great crusader, Mahatma Gandhi, for the untouchable.To him for the helpless God is the protector, Thus, those who are out caste are he God's chosen. Mahatma Gandhi did not rest satisfied with the formation of the All India Harijan Sevak Sangh in 1932. He wanted something concrete done for them and wanted to rouse the conscience of the caste Hindus against the sin of untouchability. He said "Unless and until we befriend the Harijan, unless and until we treat him as our own brother, we can not treat humanity as one brotherhood. The whole movement for the removal of untouchability is a movement for the establishment of universal brotherhood, and nothing less".

The Land and the People

It is vivid from the title of the paper that the Harijan of Mithila area are the people under study. Culturally Mithila stands apart pre-eminently on the land given to intellectual pursuits and consequently to speculations about the spiritual well being of man. The Upanisads which embody the highest truths ever found out by the Aryan race about life, soul and hereafter, record the great impetus given to these speculations by the philosopher king of the Videhas, Janaka, whose example of disinterested discharge of duties has been extolled even by Lord Krishna in the Gita. It was mostly here, in the land of Mithila, that of Great Brahma-vidya was perfected. As per Memorandum submitted by All India Maithil Mahasabha to the States Re-organisation commission in 1954. Mithila was nearly 20,000 square miles in area consisting of the old districts Darbhanga, Muzaffarpur, Champaran, Saharsa, Monghyr, Purnea and partially Bhagalpur and Santhal Pargana and the total population was about two crores then.

The land of Mithila has been famous not only for radiating the light of philosophical thinking, but also for fine art and craft, paintings and terra-cota, affluence and aristocracy. It has mainly been a land of Great Tradition of the Maithil Brahmins and of the Sotriyas. There are good accounts of these landlords of the high castes where as we have very scanty and sktechy description of low caste people and specially the Harijan without whom any study of the life and culture of Mithila will not be perfect. The contribution of 13.4 percent Harijan of the total population of the district of Darbhanga as watchmen, leather workers, basket makers, sweepers, scavengers, cobblers, washermen, Palanquine-carrier, Sahis and drumers have been underestimated and ignored. Hence, it is high time to evaluate their contribution and the rewards paid to them for their services to society.

This paper is based on my personal field work in the villages of Chanour, Machhaita, Kurson and several other village under Manigachchi Block of the district of Darbhanga among the Dusadhas, the Musahar, the Mehtar, the Doms, the Chamars and the Dhobis.

The Problem of the Study

Despite the constitutional provisions and safeguards assured to the members of the scheduled castes, the desired results to ensure their rise in the social scale and their integration with the mainstream of the Hindu society have not so far been achieved. They still continue to be in the grip of abject poverty, and unending exploitation their economic, educational and overall general style of living remain deplorable. Even after 46 years of independence and proclamation to establish a socialistic pattern of society, the existing desperate socio-economic conditions of the scheduled castes of Bihar in general and Mithila in particular continue to agitate the minds of social thinkers, social scientists and the government alike.

The Scheduled castes still suffer from numerous disabilities and these vary from state to state or even district to district. Untouchability, caste intolerance, impurity, stigmatisation and pollution are some of the social ills with which a Harijan child is believed to have born. Ambedkar has rightly observed. "This type of untouchability among Hindus stands in a class by it self..... there is nothing which can make the untouchables pure........they are born impure, they are impure while they live they have the death of the impure and they give birth to children who are born with the stigma of untouchability affaxed to them".

Socio-Economic Disability in Mithila

Social disability is a unique problem for the untouchable in India According to Oxford English Dictionary disability means "incapacity in the eye of the law, or created by a law a restriction framed to prevent any person or class of persons from sharing in duties or previleges which would otherwise be open to them: legal disqualification. Disabilitic is when a man... by any.... cause is disabled or made in cause is disabled or made incapable to do to inherit or to take... advantage of a thing which otherwise he might have had or done".

Disability, as a matter of fact is the bi-product of untouchability and manifested through the inter-actions and caste inter-relationship. The disabilities occur only in a specific social situation created invariably by two more groups from both clean and untouchable castes. For example in Mithila no clean caste person will accept drinking water at the handof a Harijan. Similarly, other items of food and drink are not accepted from the Harijan. For this reason many trades are closed for them. If a Harijan starts a hotel in Mithila, he will certainly not yet the patronage of clean castes. Thus very limited number of professions and occupations are open to them. At some places, these people are prohibited from use of any utensil in a restaurant, hotel or Dharma-shala. They are not permitted to approach any house onwned by members of clean caste. Any attempt to attempt to develop self respect by them is strictly discouraged by the clean caste people, assuming decent names or even donning dress after high caste is deemed to be an affront to high caste. In educational institutions too the Harijan children get discriminatory treatment. They have been given to believe that these social handicaps are natural. A notion is common among the clean castes about the intellectual inferiority hence in most of the jobs they are perhaps the last choice of the employer. Harijans are by and large bands of landless people having nothing worth the name of property. Hence, poverty compels them to eat unclean food, practise unclean occupation and live in the filthy and squalid environment.

It is now established, that untouchability is a notion and disability is the real practice giving way to various kinds of procedures for the Harijan. Disability is based on caste, religion and social status. To me the condition of the Harijan of Mithila owing to the Socio-economic disability is more pitiable than other part of Bihar, traditionally the Maithil Brahmins had monopoly over landed property and they held orthodox view in matters of purity and pollution. Thus, the Maithil Brahmins and the Harijans are the two distinct absolute pure and impure groups of people living in the same village.

The Practice of Disability

As has been mentioned earlier that the disability is the real practice, hence now it is proper to analyse the various types of disability associated with the different scheduled castes within Mithila. While doing so I would like to put the social disability into two categories: (i) Social disability of common nature and (ii) social disability of special type associated with a particular scheduled caste.

Now while analysing the social disability of the first category our attention is drawn towards their untouchability, their being impure and certain tabooes and prohibitions on them like their entry into temples and other sacred centres of upper castes, use of public wells and bathing ghat, and allowing them to live in the tola held by the upper caste people.

Under the disability of special type one can observe that most of the scheduled castes under study have been assigned some specific remarks which appear as stigma for that particular caste alone. For example, the Dusadhas of Mithila are believed to be thieves, Thus, any master keeping a Dusadh as a casual labour in the field or farm bears a notion that if allowed, he may steal something, hence a constant watch has to be kept over him. Similarly, the Chamars carry the carcase and engage in the skinning he suffers from severs type of impurity. There is common belief even among the Harijan that the Dhobis carry the worst type of pollution because of the fact that he has to broom the dirty polluted and even blood stained clothes (during mense) of all the Harijan communities. The Mehtar carries hight soil, the Musahar eats rats and other impure animals hence food or adhering to unclean profession.

Economic Disability

Economic disability of the Harijan is worse than the social one. This group of people are by and large landless and totally dependent on the land owners. Services to the three clean Varna is the portion in life for a Shudra. He is not deemed eligible for sacraments nor for reading and hearing sacred texts. Mithila, which has yet to witness industrialisation, the economic disability of the Harijan gets accelerated for they have to consol with the unclean and dirty work of scavenging, cleaning and leather works. They have to eat Joothan and carrion and the upper caste people want that the Harijan should adhere to their unclean traditional occupation without any sign of deviation and change. Since they carry pollution which is transmitted they can neither touch any food or water or even the body of a clean caste people. Thus, innumerable trades are beyond their reach.

Sources of Socio-economic Disability

After having observed the disabilities of the Harijan of Mithile it is not out of place to analyse and examine the sources which determine them. To me the sources could be tentatively put under three categories: (i) The hierarchical position of the caste (ii) Occupation and (iii) Purity pollution concept.

(i) The Hierarchical Position of The Caste

It is very interesting to note that by their very name, some of the castes are subjected to a number of deprivations. Thus, an educated Chamar or a Mehtar of Mithila who does not depend upon the leather work or scavenging remains neat and clean but fails to establish friendship with the persons of the upper caste although economically and educationally the former may be better off. Thus, stigma of disability associated with any caste appears to be a permanent feature in the village of Mithila.

(ii) Occupation as a Determinant of Disability

As caste, certain occupations also carry disability. All the persons of a particular caste may not adhere to their traditional occupation, for example, among the Chamars there are several agricultural labour, artisan and cultivators not at all engage in the leather work but since the traditional occupation of Chamar is leather work, they are disable. Similarly, there are other Occupations like scavenging, disposing of night soil, disposing of dead animals, pig rearing and brooming which form a compact category of unclean occupation.The groups associated with these occupations are imposed certain restrictions by caste Hindu and thus disability gets associated with such occupation.

(iii) Purity-pollution Concept

In this category various act situations, and several notions, which are said to possess impurity may find reference as agents of disability. For example, of Dom may pick up thing from the creamation ground, rears pig and eats Joothan all these carry impurity hence carries disability. Similarly a Mehtar disposes night soil, a Dhobi brooms dirty cloth and a Chamar skins the dead animal each of them is temporarily in the physical contact of some impure object, they are believed to carry pollution permanently.

CONCLUSION

It is a recognised fact that the Harijans occupy the lowest position in the social seale. The Brahminic tradition of Mithila, famous for high moral and philosophical thinking has affected the problems of socio-economic disability adversely. Unless their present economic condition radically improves nobody can exect the Harijans to renounce occupations considered unclean. In fact if the Chamrs gave up leather work and the Mehtar refused to scavenge, society in general would lose much than these groups. But it is high time to devise ways and means to modernise the process with the help of scientific aid in as clean a manner as possible. It is very essential to help the Harijans to live a clean personal life. It appears that the existing repugnance towards them is largely due to their adherance to unclean occupation and eating unclean food. For various reasons, beyond their control, they happen to live in a dirty manner in the midst of filthy surroundings and a sub-human standard of living. Now there is a definite disinclination among the Harijans for eating carrion and accepting Joothan. These may wane quickly if their services become lucrative. There are many constitutional provisions to end the evils of untouchability, and socio-economic disabilities but the pace of change is so slow that in the villages of Mithila there is hardly any visible improvement. To me the absorption of the Harijan into the mainstream of the Great Tradition requires a change of heart of the clean caste Hindus and not of constitution.

11

ATROCITIES AND EXPLOITATION OF THE HARIJAN OF BIHAR

The State of Bihar, ranks third in term of Harijan population. According to census of India 1981, Bihar has a total Harijan population of 10142368 persons comprising of 23 different scheduled castes which is 14.51 percent of the total population of the state. But unfortunately this section of population is very weak socially, economically and educationally.

Socially these Harijans are of the Shudra origin which has the lowest social status in society and which according to Manu, were only to serve the other caste people. These unfortunate people have no right but only duties to serve mostly such work which others can not do because of indignity and profaneness associated with all those jobs like scavenging, skinning, washing dirty cloth, removing carcase and brooming. Economically, they are very poor and handicapped. Most of them are landless, agricultural labour who are engaged in on a nominal daily wage basis. There is lack of proper market for the daily wage earner hence only a few lucky persons get even this type of job during busy seasons of agricultural operations. A national survey has revealed that 6680 of the bonded labourers in the country belong to the scheduled castes. Similarly, the percentage of literacy among the Harijans is very low. It is only 10.40 percent among them, which is lower than that of the scheduled tribes of Bihar.

Harijans were referred to, as Patita, Chandala, Achehoota, Antyja and the like in the various deciminal censes held in the past. The term Harijan is an award given to them by late Mahatma Gandhi, the father of the nation. The people of upper caste have always treated them with hatred and have maintained certain prejudices against them. Untouchability, unapproachability, unseenability, unreliaility and several other social and religious stigma attached to them have kept them at a distance to upper caste people. They were not allowed entry to public well, temple and several other places of common congregation. They are not allowed to choose the names of gods and heros of epics for their children nor they could pick up a name common among the members of upper caste. They were allowed names of vulgar order and one has to afix caste name with the name all these have a very deep rooted effect on the servile type personality formation of the Harijan and this helped the upper caste to exploit them. Thus, it is clear from the perusal of a few foregoing paragraphs that the Harijan of Bihar are mostly illiterate agricultural labourers. Owing to the factors of urbanisation, industrialisation and machanisation their age old traditional occupations have also lost their scope in the modern age. Thus, the Harijans have to depend upon the upper caste Hindus for their livelihood. They are compelled to work as agricultural labourers in the farms and fields of upper caste landlords. As has been discussed that in the field of agricultural labour there is seldom full employment of entire labour force hence in rural areas their is a tendency of a surplus of labour supply to its demand. This situation is very advantageous to the employer and dangerously disadvantages for the Harijans. The Harijans have normally hand to mouth economy and if they do not get jobs regularly they have to starve for want of any saving. No credit facility is available to them because they have no asset nor any property to be offered as security for a loan. The upper castes people know all these handicaps of the Harijans and this situation acts as booster for their exploitation and atrocity. The term atrocity, to the best of any knowledge has nor been defined by the penal laws, but offences like murder, rape, arson, assault resulting in grievious hurt, and physical injury and other similar crime committed on scheduled castes and tribes may be included in it. Bihar is one of the few states where exploitation and atricities of the Harijans are at appex. The daily news papers are the recorders of the fact. A look on any newspaper captures one's eyes on the prominent news published on the front page about the murder, rape, burning, beating and several other fortures given to the members of the Harijan Communities.

Atrocities committed on them have social and economic causes at the root, but when it comes to light many more motives are imputed deliberately to confuse the whole story. It has been mentioned earlier that Harijans are by and large landless labourers. Their socio-economic condition is very low which compels them to work in the fields on landed upper caste people on a very low wage which is much lower to the prescribed minimum wage for the agricultural labourers of Bihar. If they demand the payment of higher wage prescribed by the Govt. there would be a clash and the Harijans have to pay the price of all such clashes, Land disputes, forcible harvesting of crops, disputes over provision of house sites are some of the common events, when there is open or latent friction between these poor and helpless. Harijans with the powerful landlords. There are occasions when they resist the practice of untouchability against them or the practice of bonded labour, the vested interest try to cow them down and terrorise them. Another factor responsible for the atrocities is the practice of indiginities to the Harijan women. When they try to preserve their self respect and their women's honour this too becomes irritant for the persons of dominent castes and this is another source of atrocities. Another futile source of atrocities pertains to the disputes regarding govt. Owned lands or ceiling surplus lands alloted by the Govt. to the Harijans. When they try to take the possession of such lands, the vested interest try to obstruct them. Thus, atrocities are committed when the Scheduled caste man seek to secure their lagitimate rights in various matters Other factors like provision of house sites and other economic and educational development schemes, aiming at ameliorating the socio-economic conditions of Harijans causes anger among the upper caste. It has been seen that atrocities on the Harijans have been committed in groups. The land of Bihar which has been famous for so many good and various things, of late has become notoriously famous for the atrocities on Harijan. This heinous sin has spread in other states of India also but keeping an eye on the size of Harijan population. Bihar may top in Harijan atrocities. The statewise figure of atrocities from April 1979 to March 1980 along with Harijan population is given over leaf in Table No. 1 Cases of atrocities on Harijans were not unknown under earlier Zamindari system, but their nature and extent were different from the present day. If an individual Harijan was found guilty for some wrong he along was punished for this nor even his other family members were even touched.

But now a days there are mass atrocities on Harijan on community basis often with the help or connivance of the police, A few important cases of atrocities of the Harijans of Bihar are given below which will reflect their nature and extent -

Belchi Carnace

Belchi is a small village in Barh block of Patna district. On May 27, 1977 eleven Harijan were massacred and burnt alive by the Kurmis. This was organised to teach them a lession because one Singheswar Paswan, a local leader of the landless Harijan raised the voice against the oppression of the Kurmi landlord named Mahavir Mahto.

Table No 1. The Statewise figures of atrocities from April 1979 to March 1980

State/Union	Total Harijan	Types of Atrocities					
Territory	Population	Murder	Violence	Rape	Arson	Other	Total
Andhra Pradesh	7,961,730	6	4	-	2	2	14
Bihar	10,142,368	42	5	3	12	2	64
Gujarat	2,438,297	2	1	1	0	1	5
Himachal Pradesh	1,053,58	0	0	0	1	1	2
Karnataka	5,595,353	1	1	0	1	1	4
Kerala	2,549,392	0	1	1	0	0	2
Madhya Pradesh	7,358,533	4	10	2	0	2	18
Maharashtra	4,479,763	2	0	1	1	0	4
Orissa	3,865,543	4	2	1	0	2	9
Punjab	4,511,703	5	1	2	1	3	12
Rajasthan	5,838,879	1	1	0	0	1	3
Tamilnadu	8,881,295	18	8	0	3	6	35
U.P.	23,453,339	58	26	4	17	34	139
West Bengal	12,000,768	0	2	0	1	0	3
Chandigarh	63,621	1	0	0	0	0	1
Delhi	1,121,643	0	0	1	1	1	3
Pondichery	96,639	1	0	0	0	0	1

Source: Census of India 198 1 and Report of the Commissioner for SC/ST 1980-81.

Dharampur Massacre

Dharampur is a multicaste village in the district of Bhojpur. There was a dispute over a piece of land between the Harijan and local Mahautha, which led to the murder of four poor Harijans in the month of October, 1977.

Bajidpur

The village of Bajidpur witnessed a very shameful incident in November, 1978 in which the entire village was razed to the ground by nearly four hundred persons of local landlords. Harijan women were raped, one person was killed and so many wounded.

Kaila Killing

In December, 1978 the village of Kaila situated in the district of Nalanda suffered a sudden attack on the Harijans by the Kurmis which took the life of three Harijans of the same villege. There were damages done to their property also.

Mastipur Firing

Mastipur is a village in Bodh Gaya under Gaya district. There was some disputes here in 1979 between the Harijan and Shankar Nath Mahanta over the demand of ownership right of homestead land by the Harijan from the Mahanta. The Mahanta refused to give them the ownership of the land. This infuriated Harijans. Who refused to work in the fields of the Mahanta.There was exchange of hot words, at which the Mahanta's men fired at them killing two persons on the spot and injuring a few.

Parasbigha Carnage

Parasbigha is a village on the bank of Dardha river, which is 5 Km, from Jahanabad town. The Bhumihars are the dominant caste of the village. Beside them the Gareria and the Dusadh are also in good number. There was a long drown land dispute in which the Bhumihar landlords killed as many as 12 persons and injured about 20 women in the dark night of January, 1980.

Pipra Massacre

The village of Pipra is situated at a distance of about 30 Km. from the State Capital Patna. On 20th February, 1980 about 200 Kurmis equipped with the firearms attacked the Chamars of Harijan tola, and killed as many as 14 Harijans and razed to ground 27 houses, it is reported that the killers were not composed of even after killing them. They collected the dead bodies in a room, which was set on fire later on. Exploitation of the Harijan led to this massacre.

Gaini Carnage

Gaini is a mixed village of Hindus in the district of Aurangabad. The genesis of conflict lies in the location of the ancestoral properties of the Harijan amidst the Bhumihar settlement.The Bhumihars gave some land to Harijan in exchange and forced them to shift from their ancestral village to the new place. The Harijans were very sad and unhappy over this and felt humiliated and socially cut off. There was tension in the month of June, 1982 in which 6 Harijans were killed and many women and children were injured and 24 houses burnt. There were many more cases of mass murder in the village of Dhurminia, Chhechani, Dalalchak, Baghuara, Tartar, Itawa, Arbal and Kansara. All these had caste conflict mostly between the Yadavas and the Rajputs, it was only at Itawa in Rohtas that one Changur Dusadh and his followers killed 12 Yadavas.

There may be many more cases of atrocities of Harijans in Bihar by the upper caste people which were not published by the press nor did the suffering people rose to it in protect by booking cases with the police or approaching political leaders for help. Thus, these cases could not come to light for various reasons.

This heinous crime of atrocities on the Harijan is increasing mancingly in Bihar dispite only few of them being recorded. As per reports of the commissioner for scheduled castes and scheduled tribes

1977-80 the following crimes age against the Harijan were recorded in the courts of Bihar :

Table No. 2

Name of Crime	1977-78	1978-79	1979-80
Murder	10	5	42
Rape	1	2	3
Burning	4	16	5
Beating	32	96	12
Untouchability	2	5	2
Total	49	124	64

According to the study of A. Prasad (1985) there have been frequent incidents of atrocities on Harijans as well as clash between two castes. The caste conflicts have increased sharply since 1978. During 1977 the figure was only 681 which increased to 1911 in 1978. Further it rose to 2008 in 1981-82. These figures include murder, rape, arson and other offences.

In view of the atrocities committed on the Harijans and their terrorising after effect. Their exploitation has been accepted by them as a divine punishment for them. Untouchability as an evil practice is living in full vigour in the rural areas of Bihar. The practice of bonded labour, child labour, and begar are on decline but it will take time to vanish. The stigma of impurity, unseenability unapproachability and inauspiciousness attached to them keeps them away in the slums and dirty hamlets at the outskirts of the village. As mentioned above that they have developed a sense of tolerance, they are exploited in every sphere of life but their economic exploitation is the worst seldom a scavenger in rural area refuses to carry the 1. Peoplés perception of the Atrocities committed on Harijans in Bihar. Journal of Social and Economic Studies, Vol. II. No.1.1985. Head load of right soil and carcase of dead animal.They are forced to carry on all the dirty undignified, profane and inhygienic duties without proper and sufficient wages. Their poverty compels them to take loan from the moneylender at an exorbitant rate of interest. If they fail to return the loan to the

Mahajan in time, may be beaten and the little household property may also be confiscated. Sometimes they are implicated in the criminal cases. Also in a bid to harass them, false cases are booked against them to teach a lession. Thus, they are subjected to the exploitation of various types.

OBSERVATIONS

1. From the perusal of the cases of atrocities mentioned earlier it appears that atrocities on the Harijans are not accidental, sporadic and superficial, rather they have their roots in obvious socio-economic disabilities of the Harijans.

2. The Harijans live a part society, they are distributed over a vast area of entire north Bihar in different proportion. No where they are in the position of dominent caste'. Also Harijan is a blanket term for 23 different scheduled castes of Bihar hence operationally one is a Chamar or a Dusadh first and Harijan next. This weakens their collective strength, and helps upper caste people to exploit them.

3. If a map of trouble prone area be drawn it may appear that this crime is more prevalent in the districts of Gaya, Aurangabad, Bhojpur, Patna, Nalanda and Jahanabad. It may also reveal that there are certain communities like, the Bhumihar and the Kurmis who have more problems with the Harijans than others.

4. There may be innumerable castes of the atrocities on the Harijans but from the perusal of the cases dealth in here it appears that conflict arising due to possession of land, demand of minimum wage prescribed by the Govt. and protest of the Harijan to different types of exploitation are some of the major visible causes of atrocities.

5. À look into Table No. 1 reveals that Bihar ranks third in the population of Harijan but it has the highest rate of incidences of atrocity, for example, in the year 1979 - 80 there were

> 42 murders of Harijans in Bihar having less than even half of the Harijan population of U.P, from where only 58 murders of the Harijan were reported for that period. Similarly, it is sad and hurtening to observe the comparative picture of the type of atrocity on the Harijan as depicted in Table No. 2 that serious crime like murder and rape have increased menancingly, there were only 10 murders and 1 rape cases during 1977-78 which increased to 42 and 3 respectively in 1979-80.

If this heinobus crime is allowed to continue here, there will be endless caste clashes. It is a matter of shame to read news flashed as in Link "Barbarism, A Belchchi, 1977 February 1.10.1980: Janta a Belchi Repeated at Pipra" March 16,1980 and Hindustan Times April 24,1997. "The state has witnessed 29 carnages in which as many as 135 lives were lost in the last 15 months excluding the Arwal incident in which 21 persons were killed in a police firing". The land of Gautam Buddha has to abjure this notorious crime for ever its bare survival. There should be joint effort by the people, administration and voluntary organisation to stop this and restore lost glory of Bihar.

12

AGRARIAN UNREST IN RURAL BIHAR

Bihar is one of the medium sized states spreading over a total area of 1,73,876 sq. km. which is ninth in area in India. The total population according to census of 1991 is 8,63,74,465 out of which more than 7,50,00,000 live in rural areas and only 1,13,00,000 are urban. The population of the scheduled caste is 1,25,71,700 and those of scheduled tribe it is 66,16,914. The total number of male agriculturist is 98,67,433 and similary the total number of male agricultural labourer is 95,12,892 and that of female it is 24,34,176. Most striking geographical feature of Bihar is its sharp division between north and south. The northern portion is almost entirely a plain, while large areas of the southern Bihar are hilly and forested. North Bihar is an extremely fertile land while south Bihar specially the districts of Chotanagpur and Santhal Parganas is mostly hilly and forested and houses tribal folk.

Social Structure of Bihar

The social groups in Bihar can be broadly divided into six categories. The upper castes constitute 12.7 percent of total population. The second major social group is known as backward constitute 48.9 percent population of the state. The scheduled castes a categories consist of 14.5 percent of the total population of Bihar, whereas the scheduled tribes account for 8.9 percent of the population. The Muslims account for 12.2 percent and remaining 2.8 percent are made up by mostly Bengalies and others.

In spite of rich deposits of minerals, fertile land and perennial rivers, Bihar is one of the most under developed and backward states. It is mainly due to defective land tenure systems, resulting in highly skewed land distributed and leading to low agriculture productivity.

Bihar is a caste and faction ridden state. There is growing tension in the rural areas due to dominance of the upper castes together with the ethos of the zamindari culture. The economic advancement of the backward classes and growing socio-political awareness among the Harijans have aggravated the problem during recent years. It is the upper caste people who own and possess most of the cultivable fertile lands but they depend upon backward and Harijan for the agricultural operation. Majority of these land holders are the supporter of Congress party a few of them have favoured B.J.P, and Janta Dal also in recent past.

Factionalism in Bihar is thoroughly marked by casteism. The middle caste or Backward leadership is not aimed at improving the overall status of those caste in society.Their role is only to attract the votes of their castes which constitutes 48.9 percent for specific faction leaders.This group is heading the Govt. in Bihar with Rabri Devi wife of Shri Laloo Prasad as the Chief Minister of the state.

The Harijans having a total population of 14.6 percent in Bihar are the lowliest poor people. These are bands of landless agricultural labour. These people in Bihar are coming under the influence of various ideologies from Gandhian to Marxist Leninist. Even after the abolition of Zamindari the overall condition of the people continues to be deplorable. They have been given protection by the Govt. and agrarian reforms have raised the expectations of these people. They felt that Government was doing some thing for them and as such they should rise and consolidate their position. The local leaders of various parties have given them organisational help and have helped them in demanding proper wages. These leaders have mostly used them as tools to avenge some old enimity from the ex-landlords. After a period of initial mobilisation of the oppressed, collisions took place in many villages and they had fought an unending bloody war. They are fighting for higher wage and higher prices of their products and a small piece of land on which they can construct a house of their own. Their demand appears to be reasonable but mostly they are motivated by some political leader who are mostly invisible and suffer no loss, but the innocent Harijan has to pay the heavy price for this. Several districts of central

Bihar namely, Patna, Gaya, Nalanda and Aurangabad have witnessed bloody war in the recent past. There are several types of unrest in Rural Bihar all of them have their root in economic inequality. Atrocity on Harijans is one of the most common and heinous crimes prevalent in rural Bihar. There are various causes for this crime but all of them are well planned and carried on in group. This is not new thing for Bihar it has its history. Cases of atrocities on Harijans were not unknown under earlier Zamindari system but their nature and extent were different from the present day. If an individual Harijan was found quilty for some wrong he alone was punished for this nor even his other family members were even touched. But now a days there are mass atrocities on Harijan on community basis often with the help or connivance of the Police. A few important cases of atrocities of the Harijan of Bihar have been analysed before in the foregoing Chapter which reflect their nature and extent.

The Present Position

It is vivid from the perusal of a few cases of atrocities on Harijan presented in the foregoing chapter. In most of the cases there were massacre of innocent Harijan. Now there has been change in the situation they have also organised and have taken arms in their hands. They are desperate and are not in a mood to tolerate any humiliation. They have joined hands with the Naxalites. There are pockets of Harijans concentration in the district of Gaya and Darbhanga. They have procured sufficient firearms by now and would like to fight before they are killed. This has aggravated the problem many folds and the upper caste people have also organised themself in better way to fight these so called Naxalite Harijan in better way than before.

Rise of Senas

It has been mentioned earlier that the upper caste ex-landlords and rich peasant do not feel secured due to these Naxalite Harijan. Hence, they have formed senas of various type. The Senas or caste based private armies organised by landlords of Bihar to keep the agricultural labourers and poor peasants under their boots, have earned lot of fame for butchering people, setting Harijan Tolas on fire raping and molesting women.

Ranvir Sena and Sunlight Sena are an organisation of upper caste people mostly of the Rajputas and Bhumihars of Imamgunj Block in Gaya district. It has its root of Garhwa Block in Palamau district. This was a sena of Rajputas of Palamau. As it was successful in Palamau, people of Gaya wanted the help of this sena which was provided to them. Thus, now a days it has a very wide network in the central Bihar.

Sefa light sena is another Sena organisation of the Bhumihar and Rajputas of Gaya district which has fought the Naxalite force very effectively.

Achhar Sena vas conceived by one Chandra Bhusan Bhai who organised this in a bid to eradicate illiteracy from the society. He has arranged Rs. 400/- for each Block for the spread of literacy and has fixed posters and slogans on wall. It has no political affiliation for the present. Another Sena of Harijan is Bahujan Samaj Party See (B.S.P.) which has its network in Rohtas area. This has led to Harijan militancy up, in and around Sasaram. The emergence of the Harijans as an organised force under the banner of B.S.P. has created problem for the Police administration of the area, what is alarming is the growing realisation among the Harijan that organised crime can bind them as a separate political entity and can also help to counter the oppressive socio-political system.

This realition has created a sharp caste division. Things have come to such an end that a Rajput or a Brahmin considers all Harijans to be criminals, while the latter view all upper castes as their exploiters.

The Harijan tolas in the village Rampur, Barhara, Hamidpur etc. security arrangements have been made to preclude the possibility of surprise attacks. There is no dearth of illegal arms and there are even special huts to hide kidnapped people. Entering a tola after sun-set is risky as one has to answer a barrage of questions from the youth guarding the tola. The questions relate to ones caste and political alignment. It is believed that this B.S.P. is responsible for killing 10 upper caste (Rajputas) in the first week of January 1993.

Those killed belonged to an effluent Rajput family of the village of Kesni which led to fight against the Harijans. The latters undisputed leader, Natra Chamar, was killed in a police encounter about a month ago of this incidence. The Rajputas by celebrating the alleged docoits death incurred the wrarth of the gang, which committed the massacre led by his brother Mahendra Chamar. Thus, it has been seen that this type of organised fight continues in chain of action. Then reaction again counter action and reaction thereof and one incidence spreads like wild fire over a vast area.

The M.C.C. (Maoist Communist Centre) is a partyless, an under ground and an extremist organisation. It is dreaded for its brutal nature of killing. Further the killing does not have a definite pattern which has made this organisation very dangerous for its unpredictable nature. It has been the common experience that the police is not effective in the M.C.C. inflicted areas. They have better and more sophisticated fire arms than the police. In fact certain areas in the Gaya Aurangabad border area. Aurangabad, Chatra Parasnath hills in Giridih. Thudi hills in Dhanbad and forested areas of Hazaribagh and Palamau is virtually out of bounds for the police and a paralel government is run by the M.C.C.

M.C.C. extremists have many heinous crimes to their credit but the mass massacre committed by them in the village of Barain the district of Gaya on the 12th February 1992 in which as many as 36 upper caste people were butchered is still fresh in the memory of people of Bihar. According to official record about 1,000 people belonging to M.C.C. swooped on villaged around 9 pm, and set fire to around 15 houses. Then they herded the male members of these houses and took them to a nearby canal where some of them were hacked to death while other were gunned down. Those killed belonged to the Bhumihar caste.

The Bara massacre was a sequel to the killing of 10 M.C.C. sympathisers by the Savarna Liberation Front, a private army of upper caste landlords at Meena and Barsimha village in the some district on December 23, 1991.

M.C.C. has changed the style of operation during recent months. It holds regular court and they try the case and punish the culprit. Very recently in the month of June this year the public court of M.C.C. delivered its judgement on the 19th June in the village of Raja Bigha longer Konch Police Station of Gaya district in which four culprits were punished of paring their noses and ears and the very next day on the 20th June the M.C.C. extremists attacked their houses one by one caught the culprit in turn and pared their nose and ears by overpowering them. Similarly in the villages of Jalalpur and Ghirshidi under the Tekari P.S. The culprits were punished by the public court of M.C.C. this year.

M.C.C. has gained public support in several areas where people go to them for their grievances which is quick and less expensive. Now the officials, connected with the development work of Govrnment and others related with forest, excise, revenue etc. are hesitant in visiting the areas governed by the M.C.C. even Police men do not feel secured in these areas.

There are several other such Senas beside what have been described in few foregoing pages, while full length description of all of them does not seem possible a brief outline of some of them are given below :

Lalkhandis - A synonym for the Naxal movement controls the affairs in the hilly tracts of Giridih, Tundi hills, forested area of Chatra and Palamau districts. It is believed that the P.W.G. activities and M.C.C. provide training to the Lalkhandis in the base camps of hills.

I.P.F. (Indian Peoples Front) is yet another military organisation of small farmers operating in central Bihar.

Savar Liberation Front (S.L.F.) is an army of Upper caste led by one Ramadhar Singh alias Dimond a Bhumihar by caste is learnt to have patronage from different political leaders belonging to upper caste.

There are a few senas of particular caste thus the Bhumihars have Brahmarishi Sena the Rajputas have Kuwar Sena, the Yadavas have Lorik Sena and the like.

The situation in the North Bihar is a bit different to central and south Bihar. Here land grabing by landless people mostly by the Harijans and the Yadavas is main source of rural unrest. The landless Harijans have been given purcha for the land procured through Bhoodan, ceiling surplus land and gair Mazarua lands but most of the plots are under possession of upper caste men who are not in a mood to transfer it to anyone. Thus, in the rural areas of Madhubani district particularly in nearby villages of Benipatti sub-division there is a regular tug of war between landed upper caste people and Harijan Yadavas who have the blessing of C.P.I. bosses of the locality. Home stead land is more vulnerable point of attack which they want to grab and construct houses over them. They keep ready made roof of bamboo and hemp and would plant it during the night if not chased during the operation. There may be like bloodshed in the operation. At least two persons of upper caste were killed at Jogiara village under Bahudurpur police station of Darbhanga district on June 6th, 1992 by I.P.F. people the cause was a fight between one Ramsingh and Jiwachh Kamati over a piece of land on which Mr. Kamati wanted to erect a hutment and Mr. Singh opposed this move.

OBSERVATIONS

Bihar is a medium sized state having an area of 1,73,876 sq. km. and a population of 8,63,74,465 out of which more than 75,00,000 live in rural areas and only 11,30,000 live in towns. Agriculture is main occupation of the people of this state. Population composition reveals that 12.790 people belong to upper caste while 48.9 percent people belong to Backward classes and 14.5 percent of them are Harijan about 9 percent tribal, 12 percent Muslims and the rest of 2.8 are made of the Bengalies and others.

Bihar is divided into north and south Lands of north Bihar are very fertile. The land tenure system is very faulty. More than 75 percent of lands are at the hands of upper caste who are only 12.7 percent in number. They are educated and economically also much better than the rest of the people. The landless section of population most of whom are the Harijans and backwards are not keeping a cordial relation with the upper caste people.

The upper caste people were habituated to keep the Harijans and other under their boots, so initially when they rose they were crushed by way of atrocities and these poor people had to suffer a lot.

Later on these poor landless agricultural labourers have organised themselves to fight these upper caste people. They have formed various types of senas like Naxalite, Lalkhandi, Dalitsena, M.C.C., I.D.F, and the like. They have established link with P.W.G. to train them. Upper caste people have also organised caste army like Savarna Libration Front, Sunlight, Safa light, Kumar sena, Brahmrishi sena and the like. This is the position of caste and class war in the central and south Bihar.

North Bihar has somewhat different type of rural unrest. Here the landless agricultural labour would refuse to work on one pretest or the other and would demand the wage as prescribed by the minimum wage act of Government and the employer would like to give lower wages which they have been giving in the past.There is tension on this issue, C.P.I. and I.P.7. people would demonstrate over this and there may be bloodshed. Another trend is that of and grabing. They would plant a flag of C.P.M, or would erect a hutment over some land and claim that they are the owner of that plot and thousands of them would assemble for this. Thus, whole of rural Bihar is under the grip of an unending unrest.

13

LIFE CYCLE RITUALS, FAIR AND FESTIVAL AMONG THE DALITS OF HIMACHAL PRADESH : RAJGARH; A CASE STUDY.

Himachal Pradesh is known as Dev-Bhoomi (The land of gods). Numerous peaks, rivers, lakes, springs and temples are places of Pilgrimage. People from different parts of India come over to Nagarkot, Jwalamukhi, Chintpurni, Naina Devi and the like on pilgrimage to these Tirthas seeking the blessing of the presiding deities of the shrine for the well being of self and other members of family.

Himachal which is abode of innumerable Gods and Godesses is also shelter for a good number of Dalit communities like the Kolis, the Holis, the Chamars, the Rehars, comprising of 24.62 percent Harijan population, which is second to Orissa having 26.87 percent of Dalit population. The population of scheduled castes in Sirmour district is little more than 31 percent and in some blocks of the district like Rajgarh it is more than half of the total population.

We have very little knowledge about the Dalits of H.P. which is inaccessible due to hills and forest and inhospitable climatic condition for commonly being very cold. Sparse and sporadic population is another big problem for selecting even a working small sample size. In the Indo-Gangetic plains we find very thick and contiguous population of Scheduled castes but reversely in this area every one village is far from the other. One will come across so many hills while travelling from one to another village which restricts the choice of research area. This paper is based on an empirical field work conducted in the month of October and November 1996 is four villages-Shalana, Thanadhar, Baghbagot and Jalag in Rajgarh Block within Sirmour district of Himachal Pradesh.

All-together 72 families of Dalits were covered to make the unit of study. There were other people also living in these villages a glimpse of them can be possible by the perusal of the following table.

Table : Ethnic Distribution of Families

Name of the Village	Brahmin		Rajput		Harijan	
	No.	%	No.	%	No.	%
1. Shalana	Nil	0	9	45	11	53
2. Thanadhar	3	4.69	28	43.75	33	51.56
3. Baghabagol	Nil	0	4	14.81	23	85.18
4. Jalag	Nil	0	16	76.19	5	23.81
Total	3		57		72	

Thus, it is vivid from the perusal of above Table that about 55 percent of the families surveyed in the four villages were those of Harijan.

It has been mentioned earlier that the sample size for this study is 72 families of Harijan comprising of scheduled castes like the Kolis, the Holis, the Chamars, the Darains, the Rehars, the Channels, the Baris, the Dagis and the like. Since all of them come under Dalit class and traditionally they are semi-skilled labourers like cobblers iron-smith, carpenters, tailors, weavers and basket makers and maintain a somewhat similar standard of living and practice similar type of rites-de-passage all of them have been taken as homogenous group ignoring minor differences which is every where possible.

PROFILE OF THE VILLAGES STUDIED

1. SHALANA

The village is inhabited by two different groups of people. It consists of twenty, pucca and semi-pucca built houses. Some open space is attached with a few houses. Such space is meant for growing the vegetables and flowers. In average the villages has three-roomed house, each with four walls made up of stones bricks called pucca house but the semi-pucca four walls are made of wood mud, mostly the houses are of two floors. The roof of ground floor is made of wood (Dewdar).

The village Shalana is situated at the North East of RUCHI, or at 2 kms. towards South-East of Rajgarh bus stand on the hill just beside the road. According to the sociological census carried out in September-October, 1996 the total population of Shalana villages is 97 out of which 45 males and 52 females. There are only twenty families in the village out of which nine are Rajput and 11 are Harijan.

2. Thanadhar

The village Thanadhar is situated at 10.5 kms. East of Rajgarh Block and 8 kms. from RUCHI. It comes under Bhuira Panchayat. The village is situated at 1 km. East of Bhuira also. From Bhuira to Thanadhar there is no metalled or Kaccha road but a narrow ups and down path (pagdandi) is the only footpath gali.

The village Thanadhar is divided into two main hamlets. Thana and Dhar. Thana-Dhar is a mixed village. It is inhabited by three groups of people. The village consists of 64 semi-pucca and Kuccha built houses. There are only 64 families in the village, out of which 28 (43.75%) are Rajput, 33 (51.56%) are Harijans and only 3 (4.69%) pandit or Brahmin community. The total population of Thanadhar is 277 out of which 141 males and 136 females.

3. Baghabagol

The village Bagh-Bagol is situated at 10.5 kms. East of Rajgarh block and 8 kms. from RUCHI. It also comes under Bhuira Panchayat. Bhuira is connected to Rajgarh by motorable metalled road. Bhuira to Bagh-Bagol there is no road but a pugdandi or narrow footpath.

The village Bagh-Bagol is divided into two main hamlets Bagh and Bagol. It is village of two communities Rajput and Harijans. The village consists of 27 pucca and semi-pucca built houses. There are only 27 families in the villages out of which 4 (14.81%) are Rajput and 23 (85.18%) are Harijans. The total population of Bagh-Bagol is 145 out of which 81 are males and 64 are females.

4. Jalag

The village Jalag is situated at 12.5 kms. East to Rajgarh Block or 8 kms from RUCHI. It is just 2 kms. from Deedag High School. It comes under Deedag Panchayat. Deedag is connected to Rajgarh by motorable metalled road. A narrow path goes to Jalag from that motorable road. The village Jalag is divided into two hamlets Harijan tola and Rajput tola. It is the village of two communities, Rajput and Harijan. The village consists of 22 pucca/semi-pucca built houses. There are only 21 families in the village out of which 16 (76.19%) are Rajput and 5 (23.81%) are Harijans. The total population of Jalag is 77 out of which 41 are males and 36 are females.

Life-Cycle Rituals

Human life revolves in a cyclic order passing through various stages birth, marriage, death and again rebirth and the same cycle rotates there after. In all societies there are rites, rituals, ceremonies and celebrations. All these are depending upon the economic capacities of the family and nature of ecology one has to live within. Commonly life cycle starts with the birth of a child in a family other phages follow this :

1. Birth

Birth ceremonies in Himachal Pradesh are very peculiar. During the wife's pregnancy a husband refrains from killing any animal with his own hands though he may eat meat. A pregnant woman must not go near a burning place or stream. She is also prohibited from looking at a lunar or solar eclipse.

In the villages, child birth takes place at home or in the nearby primary health centre. Midwives assist the mother in delivery. The mother is given special diet immediately after delivery. The birth of the baby is announced by distributing sugar lumps or parched grains amongst friends and relatives soon after the event. Musicians play music at the door of the blessed family in the Eastern parts of the estate. Young girls and children are fed to celebrate the event. The maternal uncle of the new born sends gifts and clothes for the baby.

The infant's first ceremony is held on the tenth day of birth. All the clothes of the mother are washed and the house is cleaned. In Eastern H.P. there is also ritual of springkling a mixture of curd, sugar, cow's milk and Ganga Jal over the clothes so as to make them pure. A spoon of this mixture is sipped by the mother, this act signifies her purification.

The Child's horoscope is usually casted on this day by the family priest. The relatives and friends are invited and feasted on this day. He may also be given a name by the priest on this eve.

In the rural areas, the baby is not usually given solid food till one attains the age of about 8 to 10 months. A day is fixed by the astrologer and after the chanting of hymns a spoonful of rice cooked in milk (kheer) is placed in the infant's mouth. This signifies the taking of solid food by the child.

2. Mundan

This is the first occasion on which the hairs of the child are shaved. It may take place in the first, third, or fifth year of life. All the hair growing on the child's head is shaved and offered at the shrine of a deity or thrown in a river or stream. In this ceremony too, there is feasting of relatives and friends who give presents to the child.

3. Naming (Namkaran)

This is another important ritual that is performed when the child is about two years old. He is given a specific name by his parents. This is accompanied by the chanting of religious hymns and feasting. In some areas the Namkaran ceremony takes place when the child is one, three, six or nine months old. The parents may leave the choice of name to the priest.

Among the Kolis and other low caste people, an elder member of the family selects the name. Boys are named after the day or months of their birth. Some examples are given below:

Name	After day/month
Savaru	Somwar (Monday)
Mangloo	Mangalwar (Tuesday)

Budhu or Budhia	Budhwar (Wednesday)
Brastu	Brespatiwar (Thursday)
Shukru	Shukkarwar (Friday)
Basakhu	Baisakh (April-May)
Jaithen	Jaith (May-June)

Marriage

Betrothal (Sagai) is the first step of marriage ceremony in Himachal, the boy's male relatives and friends take the initiative in this matter. The father, uncle or elder brother of the boy usually settles the marriage. Dowry is usually not paid though this system has now become a part of the marriage ceremony. A reverse system is in vogue among the Dalits of Himachal. The groom's father pays a certain amount to the bride's father for meeting the expenses of marriage. This is known as Dhari.

Betrothal is termed as Barni or Sagai or Sotha. On behalf of the groom, his father, relatives and priest offer ornaments, clothes money as a present to the bride or her family members. In return, girl's family sends presents for the boy. Once the betrothal is settled, the alliance is usually not cancelled except in very rare cases, in which instance, the party backing out has to payback all the expenses incurred by the other party in the betrothal ceremony.

Girls usually do not marry till they attain the age of maturity (about 18 years). In the past, very young girls in their early child-hood were married but now this practice has gradually been stopped. Boys marry when they attain the age of more than 22 years and have steady source of income. Child marriages are thing of the past in Himachal now a days.

On the day of the marriage, the groom comes in a party or procession called Barat to the bride's house. He is accompanied by close relatives and friends. The marriage ceremony is conducted as per the practice prevalent among Harijan in other parts of the country with the seven pheres around the sacred fire solemnizing the bond between the man and wife.

After the marriage the bride returns with the groom with the procession. A simple feast is given by the groom's family in the village. The local village deity is also worshipped on the occasion of marriage.

Death

Death rites are very common. They carry the dead body to the creamation ground where all the relations and friends assemble. The pyre is lit by the eldest son. Death pollution continues for eleven day on twelfth day a community feast in arranged when pollution ends.

Fairs

In Himachal Pradesh, fairs are community events in which all people participate. Fairs usually have a legendary origin. The following type of fairs are held in different parts of the state :

1. Seasonal Fairs which are based on seasons.
2. Mythical Fairs.
3. Trade and Agriculture Fairs.
4. Fairs connected with Festivals.

Important Fair

1. Minjar

This Fair is held in Chamba and parts of Kangra. It starts on the second Sunday of the month of Sawan (August). The Minjar Fair serves as a source of leisure and recreation to thousands of people before the onset of the harvest season.

The main functions are held on the banks of the Ravi river below Chamba town. Prior to the merger of Chamba state the ruler used to organise this fair. Now this is done by the district administration. On the last day of the fair, thousands of people dressed in colourful clothes gather to make offerings to Varuna, the god of rain. This is done by floating minjars(maize flowers and coconuts) in the Ravi river. Before this is a procession winds through the town and reaches the river.

2. Naina Devi Fair

This Fair is held in August at the famous Naina Devi temple in Bilaspur district. Thousand of pilgrims come to have a darshan of the Goddess during this period.

3. Kullu Dussehra

Dussehara, commemorating the victory of Rama over Ravana is celebrated all over India, but the Dussehra of Kullu has got its own significance. It commences on the tenth day of the rising moon i.e. on Vijaya Dashmi day itself and continues for seven days. There is retelling of the Ramayan, on this eve.

On the first day, the idol of Raghunathji saddle on a gaiety attired chariot and attended by village gods mounted in colourful palanquin, is pulled from its fixed place in Dhalpur maidan (Kullu Maidan) with big ropes. The pulling of ropes is regarded sacred by the local people. This forms a huge procession. All the Gods of the valley have to visit Kullu on Dussehra in order to pay their homage to Raghunathji.

On the following days in the morning and evening the Gods are invoked and paraded. The people remain busy buying, selling, singing and dancing during all the seven days of the festival which concludes with the burning of Lanka. The chariot of Raghunathji is taken near the bank of river Beas on the last day of the festival where a pile of wood and grass is set on fire which symbolizes the burning of Lanka and is followed by sacrifice of chosen animals. The Chariot is brought back to the temple in Sultanpur.

The circumstances connected with the installations of Raghunathji idol gave birth to these periodic celebration. In the hills, each village, has a God. It is the village God that forms the nucleus of social and community life. Raja Jagat Singh, under the influence of Bairagi Krishan Das, who got Vaishnavism introduced into the valley and wanted the local faiths to be subordinated to this creed, initiated the practice of hill Gods gathering together to pay homage to Raghunathji once a year, around Dussehra.

When people get together, a market springs up. Thus, this growth supplements the annual Dussehra fair. Due to the situation of Kullu on the trade routes connecting Yark and Ladakh, Tibet and Lahaul-spiti on one end and with the plains of Punjab on the other, festival, regales the annual market, with the festivities.

The birth of Dussehra in Kullu lay in royal fads and it is nourished on religious, social and economic factors and ultimately came to be well-established, because of the inborn love of the hill men for and frolic, displayed in community singing and dancing.

4. Lavi

This is an ancient trade fair held in early November each year at Rampur which is the gateway to Kinnaur. The fair is held in a special level ground which has been set aside for this purpose. It is situated on the bank of the Satluj river. The fair is held for three days.

Though Lavi has been organised on regular basis for the past 300 years or more, it has a much older history. The fair has served as a meeting ground for traders from Kinnaur, Shimla, Kullu, Mandi, Kangra, Solan, Sirmour, Lahaul-Spiti and from the plains. The items traded in this fair are :

- Raw and semi-finished wool and woolens.
- Dry fruits like chilgozas.
- Cattle, viz. colts, horses, mules and yaks.
- Animal products like ghee and butter.
- Handicraft items.

Trade goes on during the day, the people gather around bonfires at night and there is dancing and singing. This Fair also marks the return of shepherds and grazers from the high altitude pastures.

5. Renuka Fair

This is a colourful religious and trade fair held on the banks of the Renuka lake in Sirmour district. It is celebrated for three days starting on the eleventh day of the waning moon in the month of Kartik.

According to the legend, Goddess Renuka lived near the lake with her husband Rishi Jamdagni. Their son Parsuram visited her every year.

This fair is held to commemorate the annual meeting of Renuka and Parshuram who is believed to be an incarnation of Vishnu.

At the beginning of the fair, idols of Parshuram are bathed in the lake and taken in the procession to the Parshuram temple situated at top of the hill. Thereafter the idols are installed there.

This fair is held at a time when the local people have harvested their Kharif crops and are in a position to sell the extra foodgrains. They are also in need of goods for the winter season. Thus, the Renuka fair is also a trade fair in the sense that it is an opportunity for trading between the local people, people from the plains and the high hill like Haripurdhar. Many religious ceremonies are performed during this fair. The people dance, sing and eat. Goods and items traded in this fair are :

- Wool and Woolen items --- Cattle
- Cereals and Pulses --- Ginger and Turmeric etc.

6. Shivaratri Fair

Another famous Fair is the Shivratri Fair of Mandi. This is a week long religious fair which is renowned for the worship of Lord Shiva. It is held in Mandi town along the banks of the Beas river. The main functions held at this fair are :

(i) Gods and Goddesses from the surrounding hills are brought on Rathas or on the shoulder of their devotees to Mandi on Shivratri day. The two is tastefully decorated for receiving these revered deities.

(ii) They first go to the Madho Rai Temple and then proceed to pay their celestial homage to Lord Shiva at the Bhutnath temple.

(iii) A week-long fair of folk dances, skits and other forms of amusements begin.

(iv) At the conclusion of the festivities a night vigil is kept by the Gods and their devotees. The main events in the coming year are forecasted on this eve.

(v) A Puja is held on the last day and the Gods depart after paying homage once again to Lord Shiva. They are made offerings of chadars.

7. Natwari Fair

This fair is held in Bilashpur town every year. It is primarily a trade fair in which cattle are traded on a large scale. On the occasion of this fair, races, wrestling bouts and other forms of rural entertainment are also held.

8. Jawalamukhi Fair

This is a religious fair held during the Navaratras at the Jawalamukhi temple. Similar fairs are held during this period at the temples of Chamuda Devi, Kangra, Chintpurni and Bajreshwari.

9. Natwar Fair

This is a cattle trade fair held near Sundar Nagar in the month of March every year.

10. Phul Yatra Fair

This fair is held in October every year at kilar in the Pangi valley.

FESTIVALS

Festivals are an important part of the cultural life of the people of Himachal Pradesh. They have a distinct cultural, religious, social and educational identity. Many of these festivals are derived from the sectarian Hinduism of the period after the migration of the Rajput people from the plains. They introduced the festivals like Holi, Dussehra and Diwali. A number of festivals are connected with the Diwali. A number of festivals are connected with the worship of Shiva and Shakti while others are associated with places of pilgrimage sacred to deity.

Seasons have also played an important part in shaping and timing the festivals of the state. Each season is marked by an appropriate festivals in which the ceremonies and celebrations are influenced by the climatic needs or other characteristics of the season.

Role of Festivals:

(i) On the occasion of festivals, Men, Women and Children put on their best clothes and coverage on a common place usually the village square.

(ii) Festivals are also an occasion for worshipping gods and deities, usually collectively.

(iii) This is also an occasion for mass feasting, drinking and dancing.

IMPORTANT FESTIVALS

1. Chet

Chet is the first month of the lunar year. The first day of the month of Chet is celebrated as a festival with the belief that the entire year will bring them happiness and joy. In Bharmour this festivals is known as Dholru.

In Kullu area, women gather and dance on the night of the festival in the village courtyard. The people of Dhaki and Turi caste go from village to village and sing and dance in the courtyard of the village temple.

2. Navratras

Navratras are observed in most parts of the state. The eight day of the Navratras is called Durga Asthami the people fast on this day and the entire family visit the Durga temple. Some people eat only once in a day on all days of Navratras and worship mother Durga by offering prayer and Mantras.

3. Baisakhi

This festival is generally celebrated on the first day of the Baisakh month (13th April) or one or two days earlier. It is known as Bissu or Bisha in the Shimla hills; Beesh or Bisowa in Kinnaur and Bishoo in Pangi.

(i) Preparations for this festival start many days in advance. The houses are white washed and the women clean the house much before the start of the festivals. New Clothes and articles of daily use are purchased on this eve.

(ii) On the Baisakhi day, all members of the family take bath in river, stream or lake, some people even go to Hardwar for this purpose. Then men, women and children put on new clothes. Women are bedecked in their ancestral jewellery.

(iii) Special sweets and meals are cooked on Baisakhi day. The socially higher classes offer food to those to the lower castes.

(iv) During the day time special prayers are held in the homes or at temple. In some area the villagers worship their deity on a high summit where a flag is placed. This is followed by dancing, singing, playing and feasting which many continue till the late hours of the night.

4. Haryali

This is a festival of the rainy season which is celebrated on the first day of the month of Sawan (usually on 16th July). It marks the onset of the rainy season each year. This festival is known as Haryali in Kangra and Sirmour; Rhyali in the upper hills of Shimla districts; Dakhram in Kinnaur and Jubbal and Shegtsum in the Lahaul valley. Haryali festivities involve in following :

(i) Preparations for this festivals begin 10 to 15 days before the first day of the month of Sawan. Seeds of 5 to 7 kinds of cereals are mixed together and ceremoniously sown by the head of the family or family priest in small bed or baskets of earth usually near the place where the household deities are kept. These are watered twice a day in order to help the seeds to germinate. The head of the family uproots the green seedling from the bed on the Haryali day and offers them to the deity. Some steams are also placed on the upper frame of the doors.

(ii) Haryali is one of the most important festivals. On this day even the cattle are rested and they are not yoked. The farmer clean their animals and pick lice, bugs, flees and other insects from them. These pests are rolled into cow dung balls which are taken outside the village and burnt with the help of dry twigs and grasses.

(iii) In Kinnaur the people go to the alpine meadow in the higher hill from where they bring wild flowers. These are offered to the village deity. There after these are distributed amongst the villagers.

(iv) In Lahaul valley, the ceremony begins early in the morning when a ball of sattua flour with butter on its mounds and an incense of marigold flowers are taken to the roof of each house by its occupant and offered to Gophen or Guru Ghantal by throwing them in the air.

5. Rakhpunya or Rakhi

This is the festival of the first full moon in the month of Sawan. It is also known as Rakhi or Salonoor Salunu. A sacred thread is tied to the brothers wrist by his sister or by the Brahmin around the wrist of different people in the village. The tying of a sacred thread around the brother's wrist signifies the affection between the brother and sister.

6. Chrewal

This is a festival of fire which is Celebrated on the first day of the month of Bhadon (middle of August). It continues for about a month.

(i) On the first day of the month of Bhadon, the villagers dig out a small circular mound of earth from their fields and place it on slab or a piece of wood. One another such slab is placed on which turf and flowers are tied. This is known as chira. The chira is kept on the outer edge of the verandah. In the evening the Chira is worshipped and the people sing Chira couplets.

(ii) In some places the clay images of Shiva are made and worshipped by lighting an oil lamp every evening before the image all through the month.

(iii) In some places or villages, the farmers do not yoke their beasts or burden them during this month. The cattle are taken to the high altitude pastures and allowed to graze. This helps to refresh their energies.

(iv) In Kullu, the festival is called Badranjo (meaning the festival held in Bhadon). The cattle are decked with flowers and not Yoked.

(v) In Chamba area this festival is known as Pathrous which means general feasting and dancing. A special dish known as Pathrorus is cooked on this occasion.

7. Jagra

This is a rite held towards the close of the month of Bhadon (first half of September), offered to a village deity. Either the deity is invited to one's house or the prayers are performed at his temple on a fixed day. Villagers from the neighbourhood also attend this ceremony.

The fourth day of the bright phase of the moon is set a side for this purpose. Fast is kept by one member of each household. After this the procession goes back to the temple with the deity. After dark, worshippers carry splints of burning wood in their hands and dance and sing on this occasion.

8. Phulech

This is a festival of flowers celebrated only in Kinnaur. It is also known as U. Khyag. In September, the villagers go to the high hills and collect flowers. On the day of the festival the whole village gathers and offers garlands of beautiful flowers to the local deity.

9. Sair

This festival is primarily celebrated in the Kangra valley usually on the first day of the month of Asin (middle of Sept.) Sair is an important day for these people. This day marks the departure of the rainy season and the people thank God because the rains have gone, leaving their homes and crop undamaged. This festival of Sair is also celebrated in the part of Shimla.

10. Dussehra and Diwali

Both these festivals are celebrated with great pomp and gaiety. They are in no way different from that of the plains. In Kullu, Dussehra is an occasion for the gathering of Gods and Goddesses from the surrounding country side. Lakhs of people collect on this occasion. Ramlila is staged in many parts of the state on the days preceding Dussehra. The Goddess Durga is widely worshipped for ten days before Dussehra. These days are known as Navratra.

Diwali or the festival of lights is celebrated on Kartika Amavasya. The local deity is worshipped and people light their homes with small earthen lamps and candles. They burst crackers in the evening and exchange sweet and other gift.

11. Lohri

Lohri is also known as Maghi, this festival is widely celebrated with gaiety by the people of the lower hills. It falls on the first day of the month of Magh (middle of January). The people greet and call on each other. In the evening a bonfire is lit in the village courtyard and there is dancing and feasting.

12. Shivratri

This is an important religions festival celebrated in most parts of the state. It falls in the month of Phagun (February). The God Shiva is widely worshipped on this day. There is great reverence for Shiva in these hills. The festivals is celebrated individually and collectively. Many people fast on this day. Food is taken in the evening after the days long fast and prayers are over.

It is valid from the perusal of foregoing pages that this study is based on empirical field work of four villages--Shalana, Thanadhar, Baghbagol and Jalag which have 72 families of Harijan like the Kolis, the Holis, the Dagis and the rest in the Rajgarh Block within Sirmour district of Himachal Pradesh. The traditional occupation of these communities are like cobblers, basket-makers, weavers, carpenters, iron-smith etc. Due to cold ecology their economy revolves around agriculture, horticulture and floriculture. The high attitude at which they live, the different climate and the marked geographical conditions have combined them to develop community living in small villages where one has to depend on their own resources, so that there is very little caste-specialisation, feeling of casteism, and caste-tension which is so common among the Harijans of plain. It appears that they forget their caste identity on most of the celebrations related to life cycle. In spite of local differences in customs and the way of life of the populace mainly due to high altitude and cold climatic condition the rite-de-passage they adhere to is not very different than the all India popular Hindu way of life. The hill-dwellers are very fond of fairs and festivals and the Dalits under study also fall in the same line. They participate in big fairs like Kullu-Dussehra, Minjar, Naina-Devi fair, Lavi, Renuka fair, Shivratri Fair and the like and simultaneously celebrate many local festivals like Chet, Baisakhi, Haryali, Lohri, Jagra, Phulech, Sair etc. It appears from the materials which are sold and purchased in these fairs that there is more of commerce than any other motive in the garb of sacred performance and excitement of participating in a large fair like Kullu-Dussehra and Baisakhi. Similarly, various festivals rejuvenate the people from the fatigue of daily, routine same food, drink and dress by introducing a set of every thing new and ceremonial including mood and mind which is very rare. All the festival-loving folk have to wait long to welcome the joyous occasion when individual forgets personal worries to celebrate the festivals collectively.

14
THE HISTORIOGRAPHY OF DALIT MOVEMENT

The literature on various marginalised sections in India is very recent phenomenon, though the mainstream authors, historians have highlighted them in a sentence, a paragraph or even in a chapter.[1] But complete research on these sections of society is of the origin in last few decades. *The Chamar* by Geo. W. Brigs is one of the few complete works on the untouchable caste of Chamars in North India that was produced in colonial India. It was details documentations of Chamars caste, their socio-economic life, rites & rituals, beliefs, religion and marriages. Further, in her works *Seeking Begumpura* Gail Omvedt brought out the radical protest culture that exist as form of saint's poet who questioned the social system and envisioned a society based on egalitarian values in Indian history. A chapter is dedicated to the idea of Begumpura that was envisioned by the Dalit radicals like Kabir and Ravidas.[2]

Christopher Jaffrelot in his book *India's Silent Revolution* discusses the non-Brahmin movement in the northern part of India. He discusses how the lower castes population in the north became sanskritised and claim themselves to various dominant identity of the past. He not only talks about the Dalits but majority of Castes that are OBCs. He traces the rise of the lower caste power and politics from the rise of Janata Dal.[3] Further, Jaffrelot brought the rise of untouchable castes from the interest groups to a political force. He traces the mobilization tools and tactic used by Kanshiram through his Bahujan political arithmetic.[4]

1. Geoorge W. Brigs, *The Chamars*, Calcutta: Association Press, 1920, pp. 7-9.
2. Gail Omvedt, *Seeking Begumpura: The Social Vision of Anti-Caste Intellectuals*, New Delhi: Navayana, 2016, (first published in 2008), pp. 91-108.
3. Christophe Jaffrelot, *India's Silent Revolution: The Rise of Lower Castes in North India*, London: Hurst & Company, 2003, pp.335-363.
4. *Ibid*, pp. 387-409.

The book *Untouchable Saints* is the product of many year of engagement and research that was conducted abroad by both Zelliot and Punekar on the subject.[5] The book was collections of various writings, research papers by scholars across the world. The authors write that fifteenth-sixteenth century Ravidas or Raidas is by far the most significant of all the Untouchable saint-poets in modern times.[6] The Raidasi or Ravidasi names are often used in place of the Chamar caste name. His temples are still being constructed, notably one in Varanasi by Ravidasi Sikhs (formerly Untouchable Chamar caste converts), and an excellent one by the late Jagjivan Ram. There are many Hindi-language books available; more English-language works have done foreign scholars than by Indian. Ravidas is significant in Bihar, Uttar Pradesh, and additionally, in Maharashtra, among the Chambhars, and in Rajasthan.More non-Indian academics have studied Ravidas than other Untouchable people.

The fundamental reality is that Ravidas's "message was plain and obvious, without arrogance and self-interest."[7] At the start of the twenty-first century, Raidas continues to serve as a spark for those who long for the "Uplifter of the Fallen, the Master of the Meek."[8] The voice of Raidas is heard for all people, both then and now, who connect with that status because of his lowly origins and the humble nature of human existence.Whatever his prior life, Ravidas the saint-poet undoubtedly lived as a Chamar. He identifies as a Chamar and claims that his trade, labour, and caste are all beneath him. He sings more than any other saint about his traditional occupation: "My job is dressing and cutting leather and everyday removing dead cats around Banarasa."Ravidas sings:[9]

I keep my hands engaged,
with the Cobbler's tool and the Leather cutter.

---

5. Eleanor Zelliot and Rohini Mokashi-Punekar, *Untouchable Saints: An Indian Phenomenon,* New Delhi: Manohar, 2005, pp. 1-48.
6. *Ibid.*
7. Peter G. Friedlander, 'The Core of the Vani of Raidas', In *Studies in South Asian Devotional Literature,* edited by Alan. W. Entwistle and Francoise Mallison, New Delhi: Manohar and Paris: Ecole Francaised'Extreme-Orient, 1994, pp.455-79.
8. *Ibid.*
9. Eleanor Zelliot and Rohini Mokashi-Punekar, Untouchable Saints, *op.cit,* p. 37.

Honest work is my righteous duty.
This will ferry me across the world, sayeth Ravidas.

Not only is Ravidas significant in the north, but the Chambhars or Charmakars of Maharashtra revere him as their saint under the name Rohidas. The lengthy *palkhi* procession that departs Alandi for the pilgrimage to the god Vithoba at Pandharpur includes a dindi to Rohidas. Sikhs in Vancouver, British Columbia, Canada, who follow Ravidas and have built a temple in his honour, have recently sponsored a symposium on Dalit issues and advancement. Ravidas has also joined the migration to the West. Additionally, there are temples in California and New York.[10]

Braj Ranjan Mani's seminal text *Debrahmanising History* is one of the hall marks and worked as major textbook for the Ambedkarites in India. He traces the anti-caste root from the Buddha to the contemporary times.[11] He argued that the Buddha and Buddhism, which constituted the most effectiveand possibly the onlycontestation of Brahmanism, are attempted to be de-Brahmanised India.[12] In contrast to elitist-Brahmanic perceptions of the past, Buddhism and its support for social justice, logical thought, peaceful coexistence, economic growth, and dynamic creativity helped India become a major secular power and a civilised nation over the course of its 1,000-year of dominance.[13]

He investigates the anti-caste thoughts, movement and philosophy in mediaeval time. The subversive attitude of the mediaeval southern saint-poets, largely inside but some also outside the Bhakti movement, a spectacular and pan-Indian site of decreased caste innovation and resistance, is described in details.[14] Modern elitist research emphasises their religious fervour, alienating them from their actual social position in order to project them as metaphysical or mystical beings who were unaffected by the material conditions of their existence, whereas their

---

10. *Ibid*, 41.
11. Braj Ranjan Mani, *Debrahmanisng History: Dominance and Resistance in Indian Society*, New Delhi: Manohar 2005, pp. 85-133.
12. *Ibid.*
13. *Ibid.*
14. *Ibid*, 134-180.

contemporary Brahman adversaries saw their unsightly bhakti or preaching as socially subversive.[15]

He launched a critical exploration towards understanding colonialism and local elites and their relationship. The extraordinary connection between the British colonisation and the native intelligentsia, feudal and propertied classes, and the consequent growth of Vedic-Brahmanic patriotism are explored.[16] Colonialism discovered in caste and Brahmanism a highly effective tool for keeping the populace obedient and divided, just like the earlier feudal autocratic epochs. The discovery of the "wonder that was India" gave the dormant Brahmanism a fresh lease on life under colonial sponsorship and the archaeology of knowledge drawn from Orientalism, and over time it went on to nationalise itself into octopus-like Hinduism.[17]

The life and struggles of Phule, a social revolutionary from the nineteenth century, are the subject Brahjranjan Mani discussed.[18] Here, we have outlined, from a historical perspective, Phule's understanding of the cultural power of Brahmanism, his ground-breaking analysis of the relationship between knowledge and power, his dismantling of the prevalent myth-history and creation of a subversive vision of India's past and present, his unique brand of socio-cultural radicalism based on unification among all the oppressed and genders.[19]

Finally, the book dealt with the conflict between Gandhi and Ambedkar, which further explores the Brahmanic-Shramanic contradiction.[20] Given the positions they both chose to hold in the political system, Ambedkar sought the complete abolition of caste and Brahmanism, whereas Gandhi fought for upper caste political domination with his unwavering belief in Varna Shrama dharma and trusteeship. Ambedkar was forced to dissociate himself from the dominant national movement due to Gandhi and Congress' stubbornness

15. *Ibid.*
16. *Ibid,* 188-220.
17. *Ibid,* 1-84.
18. *Ibid,* 251-290.
19. *Ibid,* 1-84.
20. *Ibid,* 343-405.

and double standards regarding the ideals and practises of equality and justice.

In his study on the development of the Dalit population in North India, Badri Narayan found that a significant portion of Dalits produced and celebrated a different kind of history that is frequently incongruous and dissimilar from the history that is taught in schools or used by historians in the field.[21] He also noted that Dalits are compelled to create their own version of history, culture, and heroes in India due to the country's undemocratic practise of historiography. According to him:[22]

> New histories are also being generated as knowledge base and resources for their democratic struggle for a better quality of life. This reflects a criticism raised by the communities who have not been fully co-opted in history and power...

These Dalit communities' criticisms and veneration of various heroes demonstrates the professional historians' inability to include diverse communities and their histories in their publications. Additionally, Badri Narayan noted that the politics of historiography and the methodology used by the dominant historians are expanded and influenced by these critiques and celebrations of heroes.[23]

Ambedkarite movements have steadily grown throughout post-independent India, especially since the 1970s. These movements have produced alternative conceptions of India, alternative conceptions of identities, and alternative conceptions of history that are frequently overlooked in conventional historical practises. The behaviours of disadvantaged groups have frequently been criticised as myths and lacking in scientific rigour. In his research, Badri Narayan demonstrates that the Dalits practise alternate memory and history, which influence how the general public perceives the past and how they identify themselves.[24]

---

21. Badri Narayan, *The Making of the Dalit Public in North India: Uttar Pradesh, 1950 to Present,* New Delhi: Oxford University Press, 2011.
22. Badri Narayan, *Women Heroes and Dalit Assertion in North India: Culture, Identity and Politics.* New Delhi: Sage Publication, 2006, p. 89.
23. *Ibid,* p. 88.
24. *Ibid.*

Here, a few examples are limited. One example of such scholarship is that of the late historian D.C. Ahir.[25] He has used Ambedkar's approach and techniques in his writing. Ahir works on Buddhism, and Ashoka and others are seriously involved and use Ambedkar's methodology.[26] YagatiChinna Rao, a historian by training, has also highlighted Indian history from a Dalit point of view. 'Dalits and History Writing in India' is a significant paper he also produced in this area.[27] His most recent book, Past of the Outcaste, presents the historical perspective of the so-called outcaste.[28]

The subaltern studies initiative that developed among Indian academics in other countries was unable to highlight the history, culture, and politics of the Dalit groups. Tribes are the predominant groupings that are projected as subaltern in the history of the subaltern project for peasants, whilst Dalits are excluded from this project. Dipesh Chakrabarty has commented on the subaltern past and the historians notwithstanding the distance kept by the subaltern historians on the history of Dalits. He wrote:[29]

> Subaltern Pasts act as supplement to the historian's pasts and in fact aid our capacity to historicise. They enable history, the discipline, to be what it is and yet at the same time help to show forth what its limits are.

---

25. D.C. Ahir, who lived from 1928 to 2012, was a well-known anti-caste historian who wrote extensively on Ambedkar, Buddhism, and Indian history. His articles on Buddhism and Ambedkar have a significant impact on both academics and the general audience. The article "D. C. Ahir is No More" by K. C. Sulekh appeared in Round Table India: For an Informed Ambedkar Age on July 16, 2012.
26. D.C. Ahir, *Buddhism and Ambedkar*, New Delhi: B. R. Publishing Corporation, 2011.
27. Y. Chinna Rao, "Dalits and History Writing in India: Some Historiographical Trends and Questions", in Sabyasachi Bhattacharya (ed.), *Approaches to History: Essays in Indian Historiography*, New Delhi: Primus Book, 2011, pp. 323-343.
28. Sabyasachi Bhatacharya and Yagati Chinna Rao (eds.), *The Past of the Outcaste: Reading in Dalit History*, New Delhi: Oriental BlackSwan, 2017.
29. Dipesh Chakrabarty, "Minority Histories and the National Pasts", *Economic and Political Weekly*, Vol. 33, No. 9, (February 28- March 6, 1998), pp. 473-479.

Great deals of Dalit mobilisation under the leadership of BSP have been written by sociologist Vivek Kumar. In 2004 he described emergence of BSP in following words:[30]

> After years of being consistently used as a 'vote bank' by mainstream political parties, dalit aspirations to wield political power received its firstfillip with the formation of the BSP. In the 14th Lok Sabha elections, the BJP is seeking to extend its influence to other states by speaking up once again for dalit aspiration.

Vivek Kumar claimed that for a long time in the marginalised Bahujan sections have been used as vote bank by the dominant ruling class under the Congress leadership. He also charged the left politics for using the Dalit as merely vote banks or foot soldiers. He also highlighted how different regional state parties has also garner their vote from marginalised sections without bringing a fundamental change in the lives of the Bahujans.

In another article published in 2007, Vivek Kumar analysed the victory of BSP.[31] He argued that many political pundits have given a superficial explanation on the victory of BSP. He argued that the victory of BSP in 2007 is the victory of Bahujan andolan (movement) that was launched under the leadership of Kanshi Ram. Kumar highlighted the role of long activism carried out by various social organisation and non-electoral organisation which was created by BSP.[32] For example, DSF(Dalit Soshit Samaj Sangharsh Samit, BAMCEF and others such organisations have worked among the communities irrespective of castes.[33]

The theme caste and class increasingly become the part of the discussion especially after the rise of the Dalit movement in India. This debate often was initiated by the left intelligentsia as Dalit movement counter the Marxist world view and the movement under the leadership

30. Vivek Kumar, 'BSP and Dalit Aspirations', *Economic and Political Weekly*, Vol. 39, No. 18, May, 1-7, 2004, pp. 1778-1781.
31. Vivek Kumar, 'Behind the BSP Victory', *Economic and Political Weekly*, Vol. 42, No. 24, June, 16-22, 2007, pp. 2237-2239.
32. *Ibid.*
33. *Ibid.*

of the upper castes. Responding to such materialist analysis of caste Vivek Kumar wrote with a critical self-reflective note Vivek Kumar writes that the:[34]

> opinion expressed by Dalit scholars and observers on caste and class, some point out that in certain regions of the country Marxist have been reluctant to engage with the caste system effectively. The Dalit movement has also not been able to grapple successfully with the issue of most marginalised sections while the Dalit middle class has failed to engage with the masses.

He criticised Marxist academics for reducing and simplifying caste. Further his book on BSP brought out many unknown facets of Dalit and Bahujan Samaj Party.[35] Suvira Jaiswal regarding the poor state of affairs when it comes to the historical research related to the caste and untouchability observed these trends. She writes that although there is a wealth of ethnographic literature on Indian tribes, there are few field studies of the untouchable communities available.[36] Scholars writing on the subject have relied heavily on literary sources written by and intended for those in the upper castes for their interpretation, without any help from current data that could shed some light on the beginnings, evolution, and continuation of a value.[37] Additionally, historians of ancient India have only briefly mentioned the existence of the detested castes listed in the Buddhist texts and have focused more on the study of the Varna system as a whole and the issues facing dominating groups like Brahmanas or Rajputs. She proposed the point that Varna or caste system and untouchability has to be seen as two separate reality then one is the extension of the others.[38]

---

34. Vivek Kumar, 'Caste, Contemporaneity and Assertation', *Economic and Political Weekly*, Vol.51, No.50, December 10, 2016, pp. 84-86.
35. Vivek Kumar, *Dalit Assertion and Bahujan Samaj Party: A Perspective from Below*, New Delhi: SamyakPrakashan, 2013.
36. Suvira Jaiswal, 'Some Recent Theories of the Origin of Untouchability: A Historiographical Assessment', *Proceeding of the Indian History Congress*, Vol. 39, Volume.1, 1978, pp. 218-229.
37. *Ibid.*
38. *Ibid.*

Along with Suvira Jaiswal Vivekanand Jha contributed immensely on understanding caste and untouchability in ancient India. He separates himself from Ambedkar's analysis of caste and untouchability, and charged Ambedkar for being too much emotional while dealing with the matters. While recognising the economic basis of caste and untouchability Jha argued from a North Indian perspective how both social justice and economic justice need to go hand in hand in order to realise the equality advocated by the Dalit movement. He writes that the Gandhi was inspired by the Gita, and his long, arduous campaign to end untouchability and secure justice for the underprivileged from within the system could not be ignored. As a result, vested interests and Sanatani Hindus fiercely opposed him.[39] Although times have changed as a result of the Dalits' assertion of their rights, the agenda for social justice will only advance if it is combined with a well-considered and sufficient agenda of economic transformation and economic justice with a focus on the underprivileged masses and the willingness to honestly implement it.

R.S. Sharma developed an interest in the study of the Shudras following B.R. Ambedkar's thorough investigation of the genesis of the Shudra.[40] However, his research focused more on the Shudra's place in the history of India than on their origins. It was akin to the colonial social reformers' propensity to uphold the magnificent past of ancient India while being fixated on the issue of the status of women and the untouchables.

What's worse, according to R. S. Sharma's writing, is that "he seems to have worked with the set objective of proving a high origin for the Shudras, a trend that has been very much in show among the educated portions of the lower caste people in recent years."[41] Furthermore, R.S. Sharma acknowledged that there is not enough information on which to base his investigations.[42] Furthermore, his research was only motivated

39. Vivekanand Jha, 'Caste, Untouchability and Social Justice: Early North Indian Perspective', *Social Scientist*, Vol, 25, No.11/12, 1997, pp.19-30.

40. R. S. Sharma, *The Position of the Shudra in Ancient India*, PhD thesis submitted to the University of London. School of Oriental and African Studies, June, 1956.

41. Ibid, p. 7.

42. Ibid, p. 8.

by reformist or anti-reformist ideologies. The majority of reformers disagreed with the anti-caste non-Brahmin intellectuals and leadership. R. S. Sharma's theory is therefore biassed and discredits non-Brahmin studies simply because they happen to be politicians or because they lack facts.[43]

The Shudras were brought into servitude following the Aryan invasion, according to Ram Shepherd Bheenaveni.[44] The British historians were the ones who initially proposed the popular theory of the Aryan invasion, which was eventually adopted by Brahmin scholars.[45] This hypothesis was initially developed by the British in conjunction with the advancement of sciences, languages, and archaeology.

Ambedkar and the Dalit Historiography

Without Ambedkar various Dalit movement, origin of historiography and philosophy can't be located anywhere across India. Dalit historiography is rooted with the writings of Ambedkar. With few exceptions, the early literature on Ambedkar were primarily biographical studies. This phase is distinguished by Dhananjay Keer's book on Ambedkar's life and mission, which is still regarded as one of the best-known biographies of the activist.[46] His writings provided a chronological account of Babasaheb Ambedkar's life, beginning with his family and ending with his death. The year 1973 saw the publication of another piece by Kuber.[47] His research of Ambedkar was critical, and it had little impact on the general public or intellectual circles. One of the earliest academic studies on Ambedkar's life and contributions was this one. Around 90s there are few interventions around the life of Ambedkar.

---

43. Ibid, p. 7.
44. Ram Shepherd Bheenaveni, "Production and Protection as Spirituality among Shudras", Kancha Ilaiah and Karthik Raja, *The Shudra: Vision for a New Path*, op.cit, pp. 115-135.
45. B.R. Ambedkar, "Who Were the Shudra", in *Dr. Babasaheb Ambedkar Writing and Speeches*, Vol. 7, New Delhi: Dr. Ambedkar Foundation, pp. 72-74.
46. Dhanjay Keer, *Dr. Ambedkar: Life and Mission*. 2ndedition, Bombay: Popular Prakashan, 1962.
47. W.N. Kuber, *Dr. Ambedkar: A Critical Study,* New Delhi: Peoples Publications House, 1973.

Lokhande writes about the social democratic ideas of Ambedkar.[48] The lengthy historical battle between Gandhi and Ambedkar was brought up in the social science discussion by Suhas Palsekar and others.[49] Earlier, this discussion was only focused on politics.

It is in 2000s Ambedkar become the matters of discussion in Indian academia. Scholars from political science and sociology discipline started debating about his contributions and concepts. Eleanor Zelliot, Gail Omvedt, Vivek Kumar and others have understanding Ambedkar and his contribution in Dalit movement. The edited volume of Sukhadeo Thorat and Aryama created a debate among the economist, despite of that Ambedkar remains as marginal in economic discipline.[50]

Recently, philosophers have attempted to position Ambedkar as a philosopher. Ambedkar's philosophical position has been defended by two significant figures in recent scholarship. One was a political science major, and the other was a philosophy major. While providing information on the Indian Philosophical Council, Akash Singh Rathore alleged that Ambedkar was treated like an untouchable at the professional philosophy department.[51]His later works on political theory, which were influenced by Ambedkar's notion of thin swaraj, unequivocally demonstrated the profundity of Ambedkar's thought.[52] Through his significant book Political Philosophy of Ambedkar, P. Kesava Kumar introduced Ambedkar's political philosophy.[53]

---

48. G.S. Lokhande, *Bhimrao Ramji Ambedkar: A Study in Social Democracy*, Delhi: Intellectuals Publishing House, 1982.
49. Suhas Palsekar, "Ambedkar and Gandhi: Limit of Divergence and Possibilities of Convergence", *Economic and Political Weekly*, Vol. 50, No. 15, (April 11, 2015), pp. 45-50.
50. Sukhadeo Thorat and Aryama (eds.), *Ambedkar in Retrospect: Essays on Economics, Politics & Society*, New Delhi: Rawat Publication (in association with Indian Institute of Dalit Studies), 2007.
51. Akash Singh Rathore, "Indian Academia's Shunning of Ambedkar: The Philosopher Reeks of Social Exclusion, why he is Untouchable by the Standard of Philosophy departments?" *Huffington Post*, 4.4.2017. www.huffingtonpost.in.
52. Akash Singh Rathore, *Indian Political Theory: Laying the Groundwork for Svaraj*, New York: Rutledge, 2017.
53. P. Kesava Kumar, *Political Philosophy of Ambedkar: An Inquiry into the Theoretical Foundations of the Dalit Movement*, New Delhi: Kalpaz Publications, 2014.

Ambedkar was characterised as a political philosopher by Valerian Rodrigues in a study that appeared in Economic and Political Weekly.[54] The major philosophers of the world, including Pericles, Aristotle, Abbe Sieyes, and others, argued Ambedkar's ideas and philosophy in a book published more recently by Somyabrata Choudhury.[55] With his insightful analysis, he distinguished Ambedkar as one of the radical and egalitarian philosophers.

The most traditional and contentious subject in Ambedkar studies is his and Gandhi's shared history. People have mainly discussed how he differs from Gandhi, rather than his thoughts on philosophy, history, sociology, and economics. SuhasPalsekar claimed in 1996 that the discourses of Gandhi and Ambedkar are not diametrically opposed.[56] Furthermore, he said that since all sides of the debate are vying for freedom, they ought to band together to advance the cause of the general populace. Both Gandhi and Ambedkar were portrayed by Sheshrao Chavan as the untouchables' saviours.[57] N. Radhakrishnan wrote on Gandhi and Ambedkar's contributions to the emancipation of Dalits in a 2001 article.[58] Partha Chatterjee addressed the reconciliation issue as well.[59] Despite their differences, he strove to combine Ambedkar and Gandhi's distinctions and commonalities into one platform. This debate is still dominant among the social scientist though it has larger or no advancement in bringing any theoretical or practical actions plans or theory to the ground.

---

54. Valerian Rodrigues, "Ambedkar as Political Philosopher", *Economic and Political Weekly*, Vol. 52, Issue no. 15, (15 April, 2017), pp. 101-107.
55. Somyabrata Choudhury, *Ambedkar and Other Immortals: An Untouchable Research Programme*. New Delhi: Navayana Publishing, 2018.
56. Suhas Palsekar, "Ambedkar and Gandhi: Limit of Divergence and Possibilities of Convergence", *Economic and Political Weekly*, Vol. 50, No. 15, (April 11, 2015), pp. 45-50. Also see his article "Gandhi Ambedkar Interface-... When shall the twin Meets?", *Economic and Political Weekly*, vol. 31, number 31, (August 3, 1996), pp. 2070-2072.
57. Sheshrao Chavan, *Gandhi and Ambedkar: Saviours of Untouchables,* Delhi: Bharatiya Vidya Bhawan, 2001.
58. Rameshray Roy, *Gandhi and Ambedkar: Study in Contrast,* Delhi: Shipra Publication, 2006.
59. Partha Chatterjee, *The Politics of Governed: Reflections on Popular Politics in Most of the World*, New York: Columbia University Press, 2004.

He mentions that there is a risk of appropriation in the project of reconciliation, which poses a threat to the politics of Ambedkar's emancipatory idea, while criticising the idea of the reconciliation project by the leading social scientists of the period. He transitions from the notion of reconciliation to the notion of "constellation," a term he appropriated from Peter Losonczi. Nothing could be more damaging to the fundamental dynamics of Ambedkar's emancipatory ideals than its opportunistic appropriation, wrote Rathore, "I suggest constellation above reconciliation."[60]

60. Akash Singh Rathore, *Indian Political Theory: Laying the Groundwork for Svaraj*, London and New York: Routledge, Taylor & Francis Group, 2017, p. 170.

INDEX

E

F

G

Y

Z